Contributions to Finance and Accounting

The book series 'Contributions to Finance and Accounting' features the latest research from research areas like financial management, investment, capital markets, financial institutions, FinTech and financial innovation, accounting methods and standards, reporting, and corporate governance, among others. Books published in this series are primarily monographs and edited volumes that present new research results, both theoretical and empirical, on a clearly defined topic. All books are published in print and digital formats and disseminated globally. This book series is indexed in Scopus.

Miroslava Vlčková

Controlling as a Business Process Management Tool

A Financial Performance Measurement and Management Control Perspective

Springer

Miroslava Vlčková
Faculty of Economics
University of South Bohemia in České Budějovice
České Budějovice, Czech Republic

ISSN 2730-6038 ISSN 2730-6046 (electronic)
Contributions to Finance and Accounting
ISBN 978-3-032-27525-7 ISBN 978-3-032-27526-4 (eBook)
https://doi.org/10.1007/978-3-032-27526-4

This Springer imprint is published by the registered company Springer Nature Switzerland AG
The registered company address is: Gewerbestrasse 11, 6330 Cham, Switzerland

Competing Interests The author has no competing interests to declare that are relevant to the content of this manuscript.

About This Book

This monograph positions controlling as an integrative management function that actively shapes and governs business processes in increasingly dynamic and complex organizational environments. Moving beyond the traditional view of controlling as a cost-monitoring or reporting activity, the book conceptualizes controlling as a strategic Business Process Management (BPM) instrument that supports value creation, organizational agility, and informed managerial decision-making.

The study offers a systematic and conceptually grounded framework that differentiates between operational and strategic controlling tools, clarifies their respective roles, and explains their interaction within process-oriented management systems. By embedding controlling within the logic of BPM, the monograph contributes a novel analytical perspective that connects management accounting, process management, and strategic control.

A central focus is placed on the evolving role of the controller, highlighting the transition from a primarily analytical support function to that of a strategic business partner involved in process design, performance steering, and strategic alignment. This role transformation is examined both conceptually and empirically.

To bridge theory and practice, the book presents an empirical study based on data from organizational practice, analyzing the adoption, application, and perceived effectiveness of controlling tools across different managerial contexts. The empirical findings substantiate the conceptual framework and demonstrate how process-oriented controlling enhances strategic coherence, operational transparency, and value creation.

By combining theoretical rigor with empirical evidence and practical relevance, this monograph addresses an identified gap between controlling theory and BPM practice. It is intended for researchers in management accounting and business process management, as well as for practitioners, controllers, and executives seeking a structured and practice-oriented approach to process-based organizational control.

Contents

List of Figures

List of Tables

List of Schemes

Chapter 1
Introduction

Controlling, as a tool of modern business process management, represents a key element in the effective planning, coordination, and optimization of company operations. In today's increasingly dynamic environment—marked by rapid technological progress, globalization, and growing internal and external complexity—its importance is growing not only in large corporations but also in small and medium-sized enterprises.

The aim of this book is to present controlling not merely as a set of techniques or tools, but above all as a mindset for managing a company. It enables a deeper understanding of economic reality, facilitates the anticipation of future developments, and supports informed decision-making.

Controlling is often mistakenly understood as simple control. While control is indeed one of its components, controlling in a broader sense is much more than that—it is an integrated system for collecting, processing, and interpreting information that supports management at all levels. The term itself originates from the English verb to control, which does not only mean to monitor or inspect, but more importantly, to steer, guide, or lead.

According to Fibírová (2003), controlling is a method aimed at increasing the effectiveness of management by systematically and continuously comparing actual results with planned objectives, evaluating deviations, identifying their causes, and proposing corrective actions or, where necessary, updating company goals. In this perspective, controlling becomes a tool that enables managers not only to respond to change but to actively anticipate and influence it.

Historically, controlling began to gain significance around a hundred years ago, particularly in the American industrial sector. However, it saw its major expansion in the second half of the twentieth century, as business management began to face increasing process complexity, rising competitive pressure, and a growing need for flexible planning. In recent decades, controlling has further evolved to address new challenges brought about by digitalization, automation, data analytics, the Industry

M. Vlčková, *Controlling as a Business Process Management Tool*, Contributions to Finance and Accounting, https://doi.org/10.1007/978-3-032-27526-4_1

4.0 paradigm (Ahmad & Van Looy, 2020), and in recent years also the use of artificial intelligence (AI).

Today, controlling is applied across a wide range of sectors—from manufacturing, logistics, and trade to financial services and public administration. It can be classified according to the area of application (e.g., production controlling, logistics controlling, personnel controlling, or marketing controlling), with financial controlling typically playing the most prominent role. From a temporal perspective, controlling is divided into operational and strategic types.

Operational controlling focuses on short-term decision-making and management. Its core methods include budgeting, cost calculation, variance analysis, and break-even analysis. Its task is to ensure the efficient day-to-day functioning of the company and to detect undesirable trends in time.

Strategic controlling, on the other hand, is oriented towards long-term planning and development. It utilizes both quantitative methods (e.g., time series analysis, causal models, forecasting tools) and qualitative approaches (e.g., SWOT analysis, PEST analysis, scenario techniques, or the Delphi method). The main objective of strategic controlling is to support the formation of sustainable strategies and help organizations adapt to a changing environment.

Controlling should therefore not be seen as a one-time activity or a purely analytical tool, but rather as an integral part of modern management that combines economic reasoning with practical tools and promotes evidence-based decision-making. Improving the quality and optimization of business processes, to which controlling significantly contributes, is one of the fundamental pillars of organizational competitiveness today.

In the following chapters of this book, we will delve deeper into the evolution of controlling, its theoretical foundations, key methods and instruments, as well as practical approaches to its implementation across different types of organizations and operational contexts. The discussion will include case studies and recommendations on how to use controlling as an effective support tool for decision-making in an environment full of uncertainty and change.

The aim of this monograph is to define controlling as a coordination concept within enterprise management and to analyze the use of both operational and strategic controlling tools in connection with the overall management system. Partial objectives include an analysis of controlling practices in the Czech Republic, with a focus on their relationship to financial indicators, the identification of weak points, and the proposal of measures for optimizing controlling processes.

An important component of this book is the presentation of the results of a study focused on the practical application of controlling tools. This study demonstrates that although many small and medium-sized enterprises still face challenges, such as insufficiently qualified personnel and limited knowledge of modern management systems, the implementation of controlling brings measurable benefits, particularly in terms of improved efficiency and enhanced competitiveness.

The monograph evaluates both operational and strategic controlling instruments and analyzes enterprises that actively apply controlling practices, using appropriate statistical methods. Based on the conducted analysis, specific measures will be proposed to optimize the entire controlling process, along with recommendations for enterprises in the Czech Republic. These recommendations are intended not only to support the improvement of existing systems but also to provide practical guidance for companies that are in the early stages of implementing controlling.

This book aspires to serve as a practical guide for managers and controllers while also contributing to the academic discourse on the role of controlling in enterprise process management.

Chapter 2
Theoretical Framework of Controlling

Today, business management is increasingly faced with complexity caused by several factors, such as economic crises, the greater scope and diversity of business activities, the dynamics and complexity of the business environment, or market competition. Against this background, there is a need for a state-of-the-art management support system that can provide and evaluate the required information and that can align planning, analysis, and control in business management (Mocanu, 2014). These tasks are carried out at the controlling level.

2.1 The Significance and Definition of Controlling

The significance of controlling lies in the fact that managers require an effective information system capable of identifying and addressing issues such as cost overruns or the inability to realize future plans (Drury, 2023).

Controlling provides a systematic approach to monitoring the potential of corporate resources not only in real time but also as part of the broader strategic management system through predictive governance. It serves to identify business opportunities and manage resource potential effectively (Čebukina et al., 2013).

Below are several definitions of controlling as presented in the literature:

Eschenbach (2004): "*Controlling complements and integrates management in conceptual, functional, institutional, and personnel terms. The philosophy of controlling (software) and its infrastructure (hardware) represent the pillars supporting management. They help bring the complexity of enterprise management under control.*"

Synek (2011): "*Controlling is a system of rules that supports the achievement of corporate goals, prevents unexpected developments, and acts as an early warning system when dangers arise that require management intervention.*"

M. Vlčková, *Controlling as a Business Process Management Tool*, Contributions to Finance and Accounting, https://doi.org/10.1007/978-3-032-27526-4_2

Vochozka & Mulač (2012): "*Controlling is a modern management support tool that allows timely reactions to emerging problems even before they manifest.*"

Horváth (2002), as cited by Král et al. (2010): "*Controlling is a management tool designed to coordinate planning, control, and the provision of an information base to improve business performance.*" Král further expands: "*The foundation of effective controlling lies in the integration of planning and control into a single subsystem.*"

Summarizing these definitions, controlling can be understood as a comprehensive system of tools, methods, techniques, and processes used by enterprises to analyze, develop, and optimize their operations in order to maximize efficiency and create added value in management.

From Practice: Controlling vs. Accounting—Different Perspectives on the Same Data

Technoplast CZ, a medium-sized manufacturer of plastic components for the automotive industry, faced a long-term decline in margins for its key product line. Management had access to standard financial statements, which did not reveal any major cost or revenue deviations, and thus the source of the problem remained unclear.

Financial accounting, based on statutory rules, recorded all transactions correctly but failed to uncover the reason behind the deteriorating performance.

After establishing a separate controlling function, the controller began working with detailed data on:

- utilization of production capacities,
- structured product and cost center-based cost calculations,
- internal reporting sorted by customers.

The results showed that contracts from one major customer (which appeared profitable in accounting records) were in fact nearly loss-making, due to:

- above-average machine time consumption,
- frequent mold retooling,
- a high complaint rate that was recorded only in aggregate in the accounting system.

Based on controlling analysis, management adjusted the pricing policy and renegotiated terms with the client.

Outcome: Margins stabilized within two quarters, and controlling came to be seen as a strategic partner, not just an "expensive back-office function."

This example illustrates that controlling works with the same data as accounting—but for different purposes. Its added value lies in interpretation, linking information, and supporting decisions.

2.2 Objectives and Functions of Controlling

The implementation of controlling instruments has become essential for many enterprises today. Some companies even consider the existence of a controlling department a necessity, without which responsible and effective management would not be possible (Vlčková, 2020).

The objectives of controlling stem directly from corporate goals and aim to equip management with the tools needed to respond to environmental changes and implement regulatory measures to ensure the achievement of future targets (Šiška, 2007). Consequently, controlling must rely on up-to-date data, and controllers must act proactively to prevent or respond to negative developments in a timely manner (Lussier, 2019).

According to Král et al. (2019), the objectives of controlling are derived from a so-called management control loop, which must be supported by an information system capturing the relationships among relevant indicators. This model is illustrated in Scheme 2.1.

The achievement of controlling objectives is not solely dependent on the performance of controllers but relies heavily on close cooperation with top management. Core controlling activities (such as planning, coordination, analysis, and control) must be carried out continuously and with minimal time delay.

The main functions of controlling include (Stoner et al., 1998):

- measuring progress and signalling deviations from planned values,
- verifying the accuracy and relevance of company standards and revising them as needed,

Scheme 2.1 Controlling circuit. *Source* Král et al. (2019); own processing

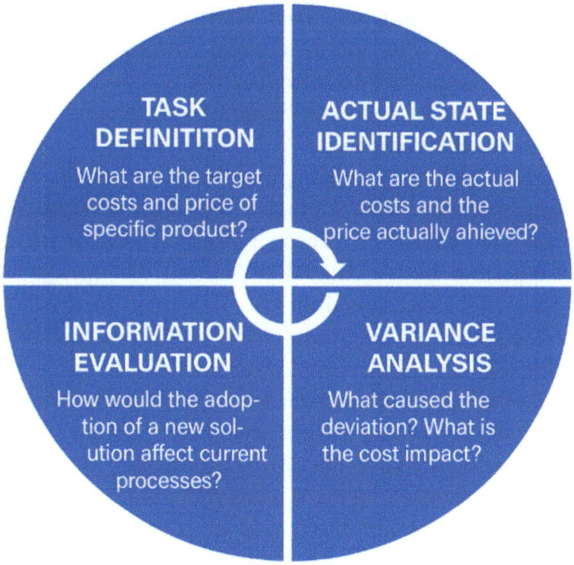

- ensuring the efficient and economical use of resources,
- motivating employees, providing clear direction, and enhancing performance,
- coordinating all departments and efforts toward the overall organizational goals.

Additionally, controlling verifies whether activities are aligned with the company's plans, directives, and policies, contributing to the efficient use of resources (Cornel & Lavinia-Maria, 2012). It tracks deviations, identifies their causes, and supports corrective action.

According to Lazar (2012), controlling functions effectively when management can answer the following key questions:

What is the profitability of individual products or services?

Which operations are loss-making, and to what extent?

How will different management measures impact financial performance?

What is the operating result for managerial decision-making, excluding accounting and tax adjustments?

Are financial indicators within the planned thresholds?

Can the company translate its strategy into concrete plans and actions?

What is the contribution of internal departments to overall company performance?

What is driving the increase in overhead costs?

2.3 The Development of Controlling

The origins of controlling can be traced back to the late nineteenth century in the United States. During this period, the first controlling functions began to emerge in rapidly developing industrial companies. A significant milestone is often associated with the year 1880 and the company Atchison, Topeka & Santa Fé Railway System, which was the first to introduce the position of controller. The role was primarily financial in nature and involved the management of bonds, shares, and other securities owned by the company.

As a railway company handling numerous financial transactions at various stations, it faced the need to develop a payment recording system and prepare concise financial summaries. These reports served company management by providing insight into both financial flows and the operational performance of individual stations (organizational units). Over time, methods were developed to monitor the performance of these units using indicators such as cost per ton-mile or return on sales (Šiška, 2007).

At the turn of the nineteenth and twentieth centuries, controlling further evolved alongside the need to assess production efficiency from accounting data. During this time, high labor costs per unit of production led to the emergence of cost accounting, primarily focused on the management of direct costs. A more widespread adoption of controlling occurred around 1926, during the onset of the Great Depression, which intensified demands for cost planning and enterprise-wide cost control.

In 1931, the Controller's Institute of America was established, later becoming the publisher of The Controller journal. In 1944, the first American research institution dedicated to controlling- -the Controllership Foundation—was founded, focusing on management and enterprise control research. By the 1960s, the Controller's Institute had about 5,000 members in the United States and Canada.

A major shift in the perception of controlling came in the 1980s, when traditional cost accounting began to face criticism for its limited relevance to modern business needs. This led to the emergence of management accounting, which places greater emphasis on decision-making support and flexibility in information usage.

A key milestone was the publication of "Relevance Lost: The Rise and Fall of Management Accounting" by American professors Robert S. Kaplan and H. Thomas Johnson in 1986, which pointed out the limitations of traditional methods and opened the door to modern management tools—such as Balanced Scorecard and Activity-Based Costing (ABC)—that continue to evolve today (Scheme 2.2).

According to Král et al. (2019), the transformation of controlling in the second half of the twentieth century was driven by several key factors:

(a) the need to integrate managerial functions (e.g., planning, control, motivation, information) into a systemic and coordinated framework,
(b) the necessity to purposefully orient the information system toward specific decision-making needs, rather than merely expanding the volume of available data,
(c) the requirement to coordinate all management subsystems, with accounting as the final and most structured element, demanding high levels of internal control, traceability, and factual accuracy,
(d) the realization that financial accounting data are primarily designed for external users and legal or tax reporting, not for internal business management.
(e) the development of controlling thus reflects a shift from reactive cost monitoring to a proactive, analytical, and predictive approach, aiming to enhance performance and competitiveness in the long term.

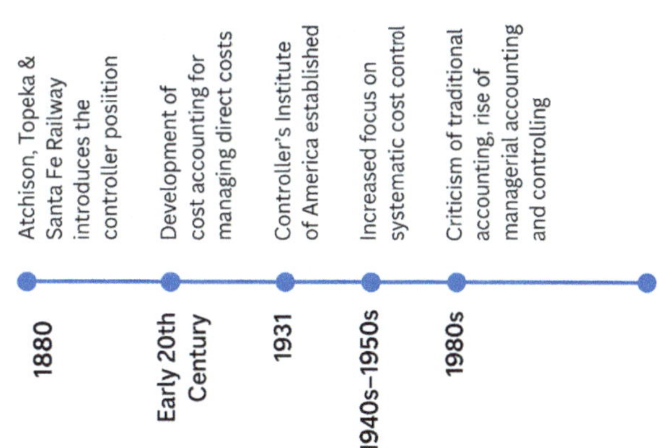

Scheme 2.2 Key milestones in the evolution of controlling. *Source* Own processing

From Practice: Controlling in the 1950s vs. Today—A Comparison of Approaches
Let us compare two companies: The first operates in the 1950s, the second is a modern company in the same industry (e.g. mechanical engineering), but in a fully digital environment.

- Company A (1955)—Traditional Approach:
  Uses cost accounting as the primary source of information.
  Data is processed manually or semi-automatically, once a month.
  Reporting focuses on retrospective evaluation, such as actual vs. planned costs.
  Decisions are mainly based on financial statements.
  Deviations are analyzed after the fact, often with weeks of delay.
- Company B (Today)—Modern Controlling:
  Uses an integrated ERP system connected to controlling tools.
  Data is available in real-time.
  The controller works with KPI dashboards, visualizations, and predictive tools.
  Instead of monthly reports, there is continuous performance monitoring.
  Decision-making is data-driven, proactive, and future-oriented.
  The fundamental shift is in the role of controlling:
  In the past, it had a rather supervisory function, focusing on cost control and budgets.
  Today, controlling is a strategic partner, helping shape strategy, anticipate changes, and integrate finance, processes, and people into one decision-making framework.

This example clearly illustrates the transformation of controlling from a cost-monitoring tool into the analytical brain of the organization. While the purpose—management support—remains, the tools, speed, and depth of decision-making have significantly evolved.

2.4 Internal Departments with Impact on Management

Individual activities and processes within a company are carried out by specific organizational units. Each unit has a clearly defined role, along with a specific scope of authority and responsibility. The organizational structure outlines the hierarchy of departments and the relationships among them.

While production departments played a dominant role in the past, today, success is increasingly determined by units that influence future performance and competitiveness. These include departments responsible for concept development (e.g., strategic marketing, R&D), customer relations (e.g., marketing, sales support, PR), and distribution networks (e.g., logistics, sales).

According to Fibírová et al. (2020), company departments can be grouped as follows:

Core Activity Departments

These form the backbone of the enterprise process. They are directly involved in producing outputs for external customers. In manufacturing, this usually includes logistics → technical production planning → main production → distribution and sales. Their primary goal is to contribute directly to profitability and operational performance.

Supporting (Service) Departments

These provide internal services to other units—such as transport, maintenance, or IT. They do not deliver outputs directly to customers but ensure that the core business can function effectively. In small enterprises, such services are often outsourced (e.g., IT support, accounting, tax services).

Their value lies in specialization, responsiveness, and lower costs for internal services. However, their performance may suffer from underutilization. In such cases, they may offer their services externally. Due to limited competition, these departments often face little pressure to improve productivity.

Their performance can be measured using transfer pricing (for measurable outputs) or budget-based cost evaluation (for non-measurable services).

Governance and Administrative Departments

These units fulfill core management and coordination functions—such as top management or division management. Their activities are not linked to specific outputs and represent general overhead costs. Their effectiveness is difficult to assess, typically being evaluated through the company's overall financial stability and long-term results.

Strategic Management Departments

These include strategic marketing and R&D. Unlike administrative units, their costs can be assigned to specific products or project groups. They play a key role in shaping the company's innovation and long-term direction.

Special-Purpose Departments

These departments provide employee-related programs—such as wellness centers, company childcare, or accommodation. While difficult to measure in purely financial terms, their contribution includes enhanced employee loyalty, positive corporate image, and improved organizational culture.

The placement and classification of departments within the organization is crucial—not only for defining responsibilities but also for establishing appropriate performance evaluation criteria. This typology—core, support, governance, strategic, and special-purpose units—can be applied across various types of organizations, including manufacturing, services, and nonprofit entities.

From Practice: Evaluating an Internal IT Department in a Manufacturing Company

A medium-sized engineering company, MetalForm Inc., operated an in-house IT department responsible for maintaining the company network, providing helpdesk support, and managing the manufacturing information system. Company management began questioning whether the internal solution was cost-effective or whether outsourcing would be more efficient.

The controller prepared an evaluation of the department using the following criteria:

- Quantitative output: number of requests resolved per month, average response time.
- Budget vs. actual costs: personnel and operating expenses.
- User satisfaction: internal survey among production, purchasing, and logistics departments.
- Capacity utilization: analysis of idle time.

Conclusion:

The department was reliable but showed 20% underutilized capacity. Based on the controller's recommendation, the IT department began offering selected services externally (e.g., installation, remote support, training) to local SMEs. This helped offset part of its costs and increased internal motivation to improve performance. This example demonstrates how internal units can be evaluated using clear performance data and how controlling can help unlock their hidden potential.

2.5 The Role of the Controller in the Company

The term "controller" most likely originates from the medieval Latin contra rolatus, which referred to duplicate entries documenting the movement of goods and money for verification purposes. Over time, the term evolved through the English counter roll and the French contre rôle into the modern designation "controller" (Šiška, 2007). Historically, the title was more closely linked to accounting than management—although in today's context, the controller is firmly embedded within performance management structures.

The top management holds primary responsibility for implementing controlling within the organization. It also determines how controlling is used as a decision-support function. Effective collaboration between the controller and management is essential: the controller provides input, delivers objective data, evaluates impacts, and monitors implementation outcomes.

A controller must have a strong background in economics, accounting, logistics, and management theory. Additionally, they must be capable of cross-functional communication, possess analytical thinking skills, and act independently. To maintain objectivity, controllers should be granted the authority to communicate openly, even when delivering unfavorable information.

Unlike managers, controllers do not make decisions or issue directives. Their role lies in collecting, organizing, and interpreting information to support leadership decisions. They are typically subordinate to the Chief Financial Officer (CFO) and are responsible for ensuring value-based management, proper structuring of information, and internal data consistency. The controller's neutrality is essential; they should not be incentivized to inflate results or conceal emerging problems.

According to Fibírová et al. (2020), the controller's role differs from that of a manager in several key aspects:

- the controller prepares inputs for planning and decision-making (but does not decide),
- reports deviations (while resolution remains the manager's responsibility),
- defines methodologies for budgeting, costing, and internal pricing,
- acts as a trusted advisor to management and is accepted as a key contributor to the decision-making process.

The controller's organizational role evolves alongside their growing competencies. Their placement depends on internal factors (company size, technological sophistication, complexity of operations) as well as external conditions (economic structure, regulatory landscape, labor market).

As the controller's responsibilities expand, so too does their hierarchical status, allowing them to influence strategic decision-making more directly.

Various structural models for placing controllers exist in practice:

1. Staff position—the controller operates as an independent advisory body.
2. Line position—the controller is embedded within an operational department.
3. Cross-functional role—the controller collaborates with line managers across units.
4. Outsourced controlling—typical in smaller firms where internal teams are inefficient (Scheme 2.3).

The individual controller positions are clearly arranged in the diagram above. Advantages of outsourcing include lower costs, specialized expertise, and reduced

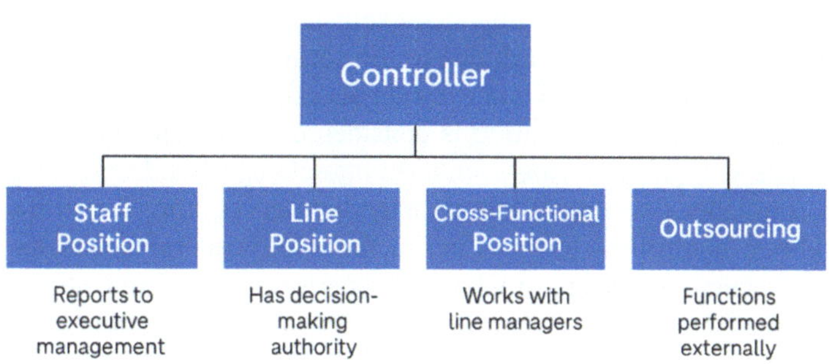

Scheme 2.3 Controller position. *Source* Own processing

internal conflicts. Potential drawbacks involve limited insight into internal processes and reduced responsiveness.

From Practice: Transition from In-House to Outsourced Controlling
BuildCon Ltd., a mid-sized construction company, had long struggled with limited internal capacity for planning, reporting, and budgeting. The internal controller was overwhelmed with day-to-day tasks, which left little time for strategic analysis. Management decided to outsource selected controlling functions.

An external controlling firm took over the following services:

- preparation of monthly reports comparing plans and actuals,
- project cost calculations,
- financial analysis for banking partners,
- methodological support for internal pricing.

An internal controller remained in place as a coordinator, managing communication between the external team and company management.

Results after one year:

- reporting became more consistent and higher in quality,
- management gained more time for strategic decisions,
- the external team introduced new tools (e.g., predictive dashboards),
- conflicts over accuracy and deadlines significantly decreased.

The combining in-house and outsourced controlling can be an effective solution for small to mid-sized enterprises, provided that roles and communication are clearly defined.

2.6 Controlling Versus Management (or Managerial) Accounting

Management accounting is an integral part of the managerial information system. It ensures the collection, processing, and evaluation of data required for business decision-making. Its outputs are intended exclusively for internal users—primarily top and middle management—and, due to the sensitive nature of the data, they are often non-public and protected from external access, especially competitors.

As such, management accounting is considered a component of controlling. In some literature, the two terms are even used interchangeably. However, controlling represents a broader concept. While management accounting forms the informational backbone, controlling incorporates methodology, interpretation, and the tools necessary for planning, decision-making, and performance optimization.

Unlike financial accounting, management accounting is not subject to legal regulations. Its structure, format, and content are fully determined by the organization's internal needs. According to the Accounting Standards, management accounting is only required to support financial accounting in areas such as:

- tracking internally produced inventory,
- valuation of in-house production,
- capitalization of internally created assets.

Management accounting can be conducted as analytical extensions of financial accounts,

or separate accounting ledger, or a combination of both methods. The specific implementation depends on the enterprise's management structure and the complexity of its processes.

According to research by Bui et al. (2020), the level and content of management accounting vary depending on company size, years in operation, and industry. Micro-enterprises often rely on financial accounting analysis. In contrast, small to large companies typically use more advanced tools, such as:

- activity-based costing (ABC),
- activity-based budgeting (ABB),
- decision-support analysis,
- target costing,
- strategic planning instruments.

Vlčková (2020) identifies several key differences between management and financial accounting (see Table 2.1).

Management accounting can be further divided into two interconnected subsystems:

1. Management Accounting (narrow sense)—provides information for tactical and strategic decisions, including planning for future scenarios and capacity management.
2. Cost Accounting—focuses on operational cost control and performance monitoring, serving as a basis for tactical planning.

This dual structure aligns directly with the division of controlling into operational and strategic controlling, which will be analyzed in detail in the following chapters.

Table 2.1 Key differences between management and financial accounting

Management accounting	Financial accounting
Analytical, detailed information	Aggregated, synthetic reporting
Focused on management needs	Bound by laws and standards
Present- and future-oriented	Past-oriented
Continuous data availability	Annual or periodic reporting
Confidential	Public and audited
Critical and dynamic information	Stable and standardized

*Source*Vlčková (2020)

2.7 Controlling Tools

Deciding to implement controlling is not merely about adopting a software tool to organize and evaluate accounting data. It represents a comprehensive shift in the company's management approach, affecting all activities. This transition necessitates adjustments in planning processes, accounting methodologies, valuation methods, organizational structure, and particularly the system for evaluating actual performance against plans. A crucial aspect is the decision to utilize market research, which informs sales policies and assesses market performance (Lazar, 2012).

The objective of controlling is to provide management with information not only about the current state but also about the desired development, enabling comparisons between the two. Controlling thus serves as a tool for coordinating planning, control, and information provision to improve business processes.

The effective controlling requires a deep understanding of the relationships between costs, revenues, profit, income, and expenditures. The goal is to identify the causes of costs and their relationship to achieved revenues. Modern controlling focuses on managing activities that cause costs rather than the costs themselves.

Performance measurement is an integral part of controlling. Performance represents the manner in which a company conducts its activities and is expressed through quantitative and qualitative indicators. Commonly used tools include:

1. Cost and revenue analysis: Provides an overview of the efficiency of individual activities.
2. Profitability analysis: Helps identify the most profitable products or services.
3. Income and expenditure analysis: Allows monitoring of cash flows and their impact on the company's liquidity.

Advancements in information technology enable the creation of alternative solutions tailored to specific controlling needs, enhancing flexibility and efficiency in decision-making processes.

Strategic and Operational Controlling

In practice, we distinguish between two fundamental types of controlling. Strategic controlling focuses on the company's long-term goals and mission. It assists in defining corporate strategies, identifying potentials and bottlenecks, and formulating corporate policies. The time horizon of strategic controlling is not strictly limited and often exceeds five years. Profit is not viewed as a goal but as a result of proper strategic management. Operational controlling concentrates on short-term goals, typically within a one to three-year horizon. It analyzes profitability, liquidity, and cost-effectiveness. Operational controlling focuses on quantitative aspects of management and provides information for day-to-day decision-making. Tools of operational controlling employs various tools for effective cost and performance management are:

- Cost-Performance Controlling: Provides information on costs incurred for individual outputs, which is essential for decisions regarding the volume and structure of outputs.

Table 2.2 Characteristics of operational and strategic controlling

Characteristics	Operational controlling	Strategic controlling
Orientation	Economy	Adaptation
Degree	Operational planning and budgeting	Strategic planning
Dimensions	Expenditure, income, costs and revenues	Opportunities, risks, strengths, weaknesses
Target values	Profit, economy, profitability	Potential for success

Source Horváth and Partners (2004), own processing

- Responsibility Controlling: Monitors the performance of individual organizational units and motivates managers to achieve set goals.

These tools enable detailed analysis of costs and revenues at the level of individual products, services, or organizational units, contributing to more effective management and optimization of business processes. Table 2.2 clearly summarizes the characteristics of operational and strategic controlling.

2.8 Operational Controlling Tools

Operational controlling focuses on managing business activities in the short term, typically within a one to three-year horizon. Its main objective is to ensure the company's liquidity, profitability, and cost-efficiency. Unlike strategic controlling (which is oriented toward long-term goals and qualitative development) operational controlling is predominantly quantitative in nature and closely tied to financial planning, budgeting, and day-to-day management.

Key Areas of Operational Controlling:

- Liquidity—Maintaining liquidity means ensuring that the company can meet its short-term obligations. In this area, controlling monitors cash flows, their structure, and timing. It identifies discrepancies between planned and actual cash inflows and outflows and detects risks of financial instability. This also includes managing working capital and ensuring timely responses to liquidity shortfalls.
- Profitability (Economic Efficiency)—Profitability measures how effectively a company uses its resources to generate profit. Operational controlling focuses on profit from sold outputs—calculated as the difference between revenues and costs. To better evaluate efficiency, relative indicators are used (e.g. Return on Sales (Profit / Revenue); Return on Costs (Profit / Costs); Return on Total or Equity Capital). These indicators allow for comparisons across time periods, products, or business units and support performance benchmarking.
- Effectiveness—Effectiveness reflects the degree to which a company achieves its stated goals. It is the relationship between actual results and intended objectives.

The return on equity (ROE) is often considered the ultimate indicator of effectiveness, as it measures how well the company enhances shareholder value compared to alternative investments.

- Cost-Efficiency (Economy)—Cost-efficiency is based on the principle of achieving desired outputs with minimal inputs. It assesses the cost structure relative to the volume and complexity of the output. A critical indicator here is the average unit cost, which highlights areas with excessive expenditures and enables the development of cost-saving strategies.

Operational controlling goes beyond data collection—it provides tools for timely deviation detection, process optimization, and decision support in day-to-day management. Its effective implementation contributes significantly to the financial stability, operational performance, and competitiveness of the enterprise.

From Practice: Evaluating Profitability and Cost-Efficiency Across Product Lines
The company TechForm Ltd. manufactures two main products—Component A and Component B. During the monthly controlling cycle, the controller analyzed the profitability and unit cost of both product lines:

Indicator	Component A	Component B
Revenue (€)	1,200,000	900,000
Costs (€)	850,000	870,000
Units sold	5000	3000

Profit (absolute efficiency)

A: 1,200,000–850,000 = € 350,000

B: 900,000–870,000 = € 30,000

Return on Sales (relative efficiency)

A: 350,000/1,200,000 = 29.2%

B: 30,000/900,000 = 3.3%

Average unit cost (cost-efficiency)

A: 850,000/5000 = € 170/unit

B: 870,000/3000 = € 290/unit

Product A shows strong profitability and cost-efficiency. Product B is near break-even, with significantly higher unit costs. The controller recommends a detailed analysis of the production process for Product B and a review of its pricing strategy.

This example illustrates how operational controlling can quickly highlight under-performing product lines and support corrective decisions based on concrete financial indicators.

2.8.1 Costing

Cost calculation of outputs is one of the fundamental tools of operational controlling. Its purpose is to assign value-based indicators, especially costs, profit, and price, to a specific unit of output (such as a product, service, or project). Ideally, all business outputs should be subject to cost calculation.

Calculations are created using different methods depending on the nature of the output, the way costs are allocated, and the structure of cost items (Čechová, 2011). Cost calculations serve several key managerial functions:

- Cost-efficiency control—by comparing actual costs to predetermined (standard) costs,
- Internal transfer pricing—used to price internal outputs and assess costs and revenues of individual departments,
- External pricing decisions—provide a basis for determining market prices, setting sales prices, or deciding on discounts and price adjustments,
- Planning and budgeting—serve as essential inputs for creating financial plans and budgets,
- Deciding on output volume and structure—help evaluate the economic viability of different output configurations,
- Make-or-buy decisions—support decisions on whether to produce outputs in-house or outsource them to external suppliers,
- Valuation of self-constructed assets—for example, when recognizing internally developed assets or capitalized in-house investments (Čechová, 2011).

All these functions are not performed by a single calculation but rather by an interconnected calculation system, composed of several different types of cost calculations. These calculations differ in their structure and included cost items, and in the approach, they use for example, additive costing (cost-based) or retrograde costing, which starts from the final target price and works backward (Scheme 2.4).

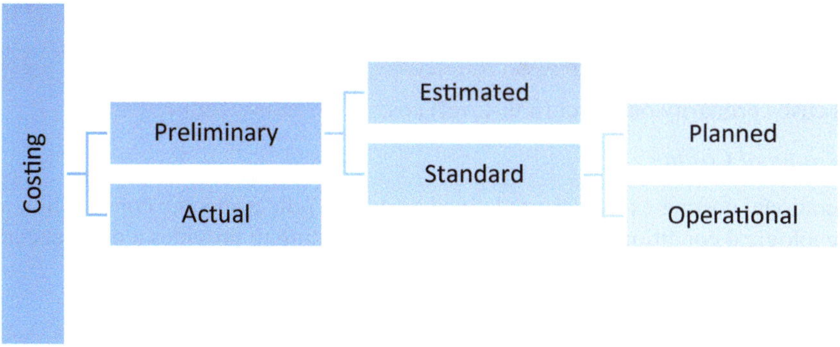

Scheme 2.4 Costing system. *Source* Own processing

From the above scheme, it is evident that cost calculations are categorized based on their time horizon into preliminary and final costings. Preliminary calculations are prepared prior to the actual execution of production and serve their purpose in the planning phase. These are further subdivided by their purpose and method into estimated, operational, and planned calculations. Operational and planned costings together form what is known as norm-based calculations. In contrast, final costings are compiled only after the performance is completed or the product is sold. Types of costing are defined as follows:

Estimated Costing

This type is typically prepared during the research, development, and pre-production phases, when neither manufacturing nor sales have started. It evaluates future expected costs of performance based on assumed features and technical parameters, aiming to ensure that both costs and pricing will yield the desired profit.

Estimated costing becomes particularly important at the end of the development phase, right before the start of technical and technological preparation for production. At this stage, it serves as a cost limit for production preparation departments.

In contract-based operations, it reflects the cost intensity of the individual output and forms the basis for pricing negotiations. Estimated costing is typically prepared using full cost accounting, including allocations for sales and administrative overheads. A retrograde costing formula is recommended to verify that the price covers all costs and includes a profit margin.

Planned Costing

Planned costing is prepared for a specific budget period and represents the targeted cost level that should be achieved during that period. It is especially useful for repetitive production over an extended timeframe. In project- or order-based activities, its role is often fulfilled by operational costing.

Planned costings are developed once technical norms are known, based on current production conditions, including product specifications and technological processes. This type of costing can take two forms:

- Partial-period planning (e.g., monthly),
- Entire budget period planning.

It focuses primarily on direct (unit-level) costs.

Operational Costing

Operational costing expresses predefined costs that reflect specific construction and technological conditions. Compared to planned costing, it provides a more accurate estimation based on real-time, concrete conditions.

It also exists in two forms:

- Operational costing for a part of the period,
- Operational costing for the entire monitored period.

This calculation is typically used for material costs, based on material consumption norms and unit prices, and for direct labor, based on time-based performance norms and wage rates per time unit.

Final Costing

Final costing reflects the actual costs incurred (or average actual costs) per unit produced in a particular period or batch. When compared with operational costing, it becomes a crucial tool for controlling cost efficiency, especially in the use of direct costs.

This form of costing is most frequently applied in contract-type operations or long production cycles. It is generally developed using full cost accounting with the goal of determining the true costs of the final performance or product.

Cost Classification

As previously discussed, there exists a comprehensive system of cost calculations, where each calculation may differ based on the types of costs included, the formula applied, or the time frame considered. Therefore, costs must be classified according to various criteria or groupings. The first fundamental question when tracking costs is understanding their economic nature at the moment they enter the enterprise. From this perspective, costs are divided into natural (by type) and functional (by purpose) classifications.

The natural classification of costs is characterized as being primary, external, and simple, with limited potential for further breakdown. The basic categories in this classification include:

- Consumption of materials and energy,
- Services,
- Wage costs,
- Depreciation,
- Financial costs.

The advantage of this classification lies in its clarity and traceability, ensuring unambiguous reporting of consumption. However, it does not explain the purpose behind incurring the costs that is, the relationship to the performed outputs. This shortcoming is addressed by the functional classification of costs.

The functional classification focuses on understanding the causes of resource consumption. It can be further divided into the following categories (Fibírová et al., 2020; Král et al., 2019; Popesko, 2009):

Technological Costs vs. Service and Management Costs

The dividing criterion here is whether the cost is related to the execution and organization of the activity or directly to the production of outputs.

Technological costs are incurred during the creation of outputs and are determined by the technology of the activity. Examples include consumption of raw materials, wages of operational workers, energy usage for production equipment, and equipment depreciation.

Service and management costs are incurred to establish, maintain, and ensure smooth production conditions, for example, building operation, heating, lighting, cleaning, security, and salaries of managerial staff.

While technological costs are directly linked to specific outputs, service and management costs support the production process and are relatively independent of output volume.

Direct vs. Overhead Costs

This is a more detailed classification of technological and service/management costs. Overhead costs always fall under service and management functions. Technological costs can include both direct and overhead costs.

Direct costs are traceable to a single unit of output, and a cost target can be determined using consumption standards, which are then priced. This results in a unit cost calculation, a key tool in managing the efficiency of direct costs.

Overhead costs, in contrast, cannot be directly assigned to a specific output. Their control is achieved through overhead budgeting.

Direct vs. Indirect Costs

Direct costs can be clearly assigned to a specific type of output. Indirect costs contribute to the creation of conditions for a group of outputs. This classification is crucial for cost calculations and is influenced by the need for transparency and decision-making accuracy.

Besides direct unit costs, some overhead costs can also be direct, provided they relate solely to a given type of output and their share can be calculated — e.g., depreciation, R&D expenses, or technical preparation costs.

Indirect costs are allocated to outputs using cost allocation methods such as cost drivers or activity-based costing.

Variable vs. Fixed Costs

Variable costs change with the volume of output. They fluctuate in proportion to production levels and include expenses like raw materials or production wages.

Fixed costs remain stable over a given period and provide the capacity required for production. They are often referred to as potential costs, since they are incurred once for a specific time frame, regardless of actual output volume.

Cost Allocation Methods

Direct costs can be assigned to a cost unit (calculation unit) at the time they are incurred, using accounting data. This is done by dividing the total amount of direct costs by the number of produced units. However, the challenge arises when it comes to the allocation of indirect costs.

For indirect cost allocation, the ideal approach is to determine a causal relationship between costs and outputs. Where no such direct relationship exists—especially in cases where costs are more related to the management of the enterprise than to production itself—the principle of cost-bearing capacity (ability-to-bear principle) is applied.

Indirect costs are associated with supporting a group of outputs. Several costing methods can be used to allocate indirect costs effectively (Popesko, 2009):

1. Simple Division Method
   This method allocates costs to outputs based purely on quantity. The cost distribution is determined by the volume of outputs, which is appropriate when a department delivers outputs of approximately equal cost intensity.
2. Equivalent Unit Method (Proportional Division)
   In this method, joint costs are allocated to outputs based on equivalent units, which reflect differing cost intensities across various outputs. Each type of product is assigned a coefficient (equivalence number) representing its relative cost level compared to a base product. This allows for more accurate differentiation in cost allocation.
3. Overhead (Markup) Costing Method
   This method allocates costs using allocation bases (cost drivers). Two main approaches exist:
   (a) Single-rate (summation) overhead costing—Here, all indirect costs are allocated based on a single cost driver (e.g., direct labor hours, machine hours). It assumes that all indirect costs vary proportionally with one variable.
   (b) Multiple-rate (differentiated) overhead costing—This refined method uses different cost drivers for different groups of indirect costs. Allocation bases are selected based on an analysis of the causal relationships between specific cost groups and their respective bases. These allocation bases may be physical (e.g., labor hours, machine hours) or monetary (e.g., direct wages, material costs).

From Practice: Allocation Methods—Surcharge Method in an Engineering Company

A mid-sized engineering company producing custom machine parts decided to improve the accuracy of cost allocation for their production lines. Initially, the company applied the single overhead surcharge method using direct labor hours as the allocation base for all indirect costs.

However, they noticed discrepancies in profitability analysis between product types with vastly different requirements for machine use and supervision. In response, they implemented the differentiated surcharge method—applying:

- machine hours for machine-related overhead,
- direct labor costs for administrative overhead,
- and floor space for facility costs.

As a result, the management gained more realistic product cost data. It revealed that one previously "profitable" product line had been heavily subsidized by others. The new method helped eliminate cross-subsidization and supported more informed decisions about product pricing and production priorities.

Absorption (Full) Costing and Marginal (Variable) Costing

The term Full Costing is also referred to as Absorption Costing, because it includes (or "absorbs") all direct and indirect costs into the cost of a unit of output.

The term Variable Costing is often referred to as Marginal Costing (especially in British English), as it focuses on the marginal (incremental) costs associated with additional production.

Absorption Costing assigns all costs incurred in the creation of a product or service—including both direct and indirect costs—to the unit of output. These costs include direct materials, direct labor, and allocated overheads (Drury, 2023). This costing method provides a static representation of calculated cost figures and is suitable only when the volume and mix of products remain stable.

It is not an ideal basis for decision-making regarding product mix, minimum selling prices, or assessing the profitability of individual products. One limitation is that the actual amount of full costs is often determined only with a time delay. Nevertheless, full costing remains important for pricing strategy decisions, competitiveness assessment, and for profitability comparisons between individual outputs (Fibírová et al., 2020).

Marginal Costing is used to meet management's need for information about product pricing as well as insight into which costs are not directly incurred in ongoing operations. Unlike full costing, cost classification is not based on direct vs. indirect, but rather on variable vs. fixed costs, emphasizing the causal relationship of cost origin.

The objective of this method is not to calculate total product cost, but rather to determine the contribution margin and profit. The contribution margin is analyzed both in relation to the product's price and its cost structure. The link between product cost and price is typically structured using a retrograde (backward) calculation, where the profit margin is derived from price minus variable costs. You can see Comparison of Absorption Costing and Marginal Costing in Table 2.3.

From Practice: Absorption Costing vs. Marginal Costing in Quotation Decision-Making

Two manufacturing companies received similar custom orders requiring urgent production.

Company A used absorption costing and calculated the price based on total costs, including allocated fixed overheads.

Table 2.3 Comparison of absorption costing and marginal costing

Aspect	Absorption costing	Marginal costing
Definition	Assigns all costs (variable and fixed) to the product	Assigns only variable costs to the product; fixed costs are treated as period costs
Cost components	Includes direct costs and allocated fixed overheads	Includes only variable costs (direct materials, labor, variable overhead)
Decision-making	Less useful for short-term decisions due to inclusion of fixed costs	More suitable for short-term decision-making
Profitability analysis	Can obscure contribution margin, making profitability comparisons harder	Clearly shows contribution margin for each product
Inventory valuation	Higher, as fixed manufacturing overhead is capitalized in inventory	Lower, as fixed costs are expensed in the period
Income statement impact	Profits can vary depending on inventory changes	Profits are more stable and reflect actual sales performance
Suitability	Preferred for external financial reporting	Better for internal decision-making and control
Complexity	Can be complex due to fixed cost allocation	Simpler and more transparent

Source Own processing

Company B used marginal costing and based their price on variable costs plus contribution margin.

Company A declined the order, judging it unprofitable due to high full cost per unit.

Company B accepted it, recognizing it would still cover variable costs and contribute to overhead absorption, despite a lower profit margin.

Ultimately, Company B strengthened its customer relationship and increased utilization of its production capacity without incurring additional fixed costs. Company A later revised its costing approach for similar orders.

Joint Product Costing

Joint production refers to a process in which a specific combination of inputs results in at least two outputs in a fixed or limited ratio, with minimal ability to influence their proportional relationship. In joint production, the outputs are categorized into main products, by-products, and waste.

- Main products are the primary outputs and the intended result of the production process.

- By-products are outputs that inevitably arise during production but are not the primary goal.
- Waste includes unintended or residual outputs that may be sold or further processed but generally have minimal value in relation to the other products.

The costs associated with these products are common to all and are referred to as joint costs (Král et al., 2010). The allocation of joint costs is a complex task. It is necessary for the valuation of internally produced inventory in financial accounting, price justification, and performance valuation within enterprise value management.

There are two basic methodological approaches to allocating joint costs:

- Value-based allocation methods, which use value indicators as allocation bases (e.g., sales price, revenue, contribution to sales).
- Physical-based allocation methods, which use physical indicators (e.g., volume, weight).

When physical units are used, most costs tend to be allocated to the product with the highest share of physical output. By-product valuation can be carried out in two ways:

- Additive method: By-products are treated similarly to the main product and valued accordingly.
- Deductive method: Revenue from the sale of the by-product is treated as a reduction of the total joint costs.

From Practice: Joint Costing in Dairy Production
A dairy company produces milk, cream, and whey from raw milk. All three are joint outputs of the same production process.

To value these outputs for internal and financial reporting, the company used the net realizable value method with deduction (the offset method).

It calculated the market value of cream and whey and deducted the expected revenue from their sales from the total joint cost. The remaining costs were then assigned to milk as the main product.

This method provided a clear picture of cost absorption, prevented overvaluation of by-products, and aligned the product costing system with the financial reality of the market. It also served as the basis for setting transfer prices between processing and packaging departments.

Activity-Based Costing (ABC)

Activity-Based Costing (ABC) aims to identify the true causes of cost generation. Its core principle is the allocation of overhead costs to specific activities performed, and through these activities, the costs are subsequently assigned to individual cost objects (Popesko, 2009).

Although this method is demanding in terms of the volume of data required, the ABC system—based on the analysis of the relationship between costs and activities—offers valuable insights. In some cases, its results expand the scope of application beyond operational use, supporting tactical and strategic planning and decision-making (Král et al., 2019). When applied, ABC provides a wide array of information about costs, processes, activities, outputs, and cost objects (Popesko, 2009).

Steps in constructing an ABC-based cost calculation (Král et al., 2019):

1. Define homogeneous cost groups, which are characterized by their relationship to the activities that trigger the incurrence of these costs.
2. Identify the cost drivers, i.e., the cause of the cost generation, and express them using relevant activity measures.
3. Determine the total level of each homogeneous cost group and the scope of the corresponding cost driver.
4. Calculate the cost per unit of the cost driver.
5. Assess the extent to which each cost driver is utilized by the specific costed products or services.
6. Assign the average costs of each activity to the cost object or product unit being calculated.

2.8.2 System of Plans and Budgets

Plans and budgets are directly linked to cost calculations. They can be both short-term and long-term, and when preparing them, it is necessary to consider:

- the time period or quantity of output the company's capacity can cover,
- expectations regarding future investments,
- the maximum level of costs the company can incur without entering an undesirable financial situation,
- the company's goals for the upcoming periods, whether they are achievable and under what conditions (Čechová, 2011).

> In contrast, budgets take a more specific form, as they are prepared for a defined period of time. They are based not only on estimated figures but also on calculated values and set monetary indicators and concrete tasks (Čechová, 2011).

The most challenging task when preparing a budget is aligning the objectives and expectations of individual departments or cost centers (Fotr, 2012). Strategic controlling plays an important role by providing information on expected market demand trends, input and output prices, and cost intensity. The main objective of the budget is to quantify the development of key financial metrics—costs, revenues, profit, assets, liabilities, income, and expenditures.

The overarching document is the corporate or master budget, which quantifies:

- the expected future financial result in the budgeted income statement,
- the changes in cash flows in the budgeted cash flow statement,
- and the financial position of the company in the budgeted balance sheet (Fibírová et al., 2020; Lazar, 2012).

These financial statements are discussed in more detail in the chapter "Controlling Reports." The preparation of short-term budgets is based on strategic controlling goals and existing conditions. These are subsequently allocated to partial goals and tasks of individual departments or centers.

According to Král et al. (2010), the main functions of a budget include:

- Planning Function—It sets the goals for the development of financial metrics during a given period, aligned with the company's strategic goals.
- Coordination—It coordinates the activities and cooperation of internal departments.
- Motivation—It motivates managers of individual organizational units.
- Control—It serves as a tool to compare actual development with budgeted levels of costs.
- Performance Measurement—It measures the performance of internal company units. For proper assessment, results should be compared among similar units.

Budget Preparation Process

The process of preparing a budget includes the following steps:

1. Defining the company's budgeting policy and basic development directions—This is influenced by planned changes in the so-called marketing mix, intentions to expand or limit outputs, planned technical and technological changes, macroeconomic influences, and competition. It is essential to be well-acquainted with strategic goals and policies.
2. Identifying performance-limiting factors—These are usually market demand, but may also include production capacity, workforce structure and adaptability, etc.
3. Preparing the revenue budget—Based on the sales plan for specific products or services and their predetermined selling prices.
4. Defining the basic cost budget structure—This is based on the classification of costs into variable and fixed, and the so-called tiered classification of fixed costs in line with the hierarchical structure of activities and departments.
5. Preparing the budgeted income statement.
6. Initial stage of departmental budget preparation—The bottom-up approach means that the budget is prepared at the lowest management level and coordinated and refined at higher levels. The top-down approach is used during the approval process.
7. Coordination and revision of departmental budgets and their acceptance—Budgets are once again submitted bottom-up, repeatedly, until they are coordinated and accepted by all stakeholders.
8. Compilation and approval of the company-wide budget and final approval of departmental budgets.

From Practice: Budgeting in a Manufacturing Company
A mid-sized manufacturer of heating equipment faced pressure to better align production planning with market demand and internal capacities. To respond, the company implemented a bottom-up budgeting system integrated with its strategic goals and capacity constraints.

Step 1—Sales Budget.

Each regional sales office prepared a sales forecast based on historical data, market trends, and competitor analysis. These forecasts were consolidated to form a company-wide revenue plan.

Step 2—Production Budget and Capacity Check.

The production department used the sales budget to define production volumes, which were compared to the plant's technical and labor capacities. Bottlenecks in assembly led to scheduling adjustments and outsourcing of selected components.

Step 3—Cost Budgets.

Cost center managers prepared flexible budgets broken down into:
- variable costs (materials, direct labor),
- fixed costs (depreciation, supervision),
- linked to expected production volumes.

Step 4—Master Budget.

The master budget included a budgeted income statement, cash flow forecast, and balance sheet projection. Scenario planning was used to test sensitivity to material price fluctuations.

Results:

As a result of the newly implemented budgeting system, the company experienced improved coordination between departments, particularly between sales, production, and procurement. This alignment enabled clearer communication of expectations and priorities.

Additionally, the company was able to identify resource conflicts more quickly, such as production bottlenecks or material shortages, allowing for timely adjustments to schedules and sourcing strategies.

The new approach also led to more accurate cash flow planning, as expenditures were better timed in accordance with the production plan and anticipated revenues.

Lastly, by synchronizing production with actual demand, the company significantly reduced the need for overtime and last-minute urgent orders, which had previously strained both personnel and finances.

Budget Control

Budget control can be performed using:

- Fixed budgets—Actual costs are compared with predefined budgeted costs. This approach is used to monitor cost centers where output is undefined or not measurable.

- Flexible (adjusted) budgets—These recalculate the originally budgeted variable costs based on the actual volume and structure of output. Fixed costs remain unchanged at the budgeted level. This method is used to evaluate internal departments that do not decide on capacity utilization and are not incentivized to increase output volume.
- Linear flexible budgets—These adjust total budgeted costs according to the actual volume and structure of output. They are used to evaluate departments that are able to make decisions about capacity utilization and are motivated to increase output volumes (Lazar, 2012).

2.8.3 Pricing Decisions

Pricing decisions are a specific type of managerial decision-making focused on determining what level of cost for a product or service is still acceptable and what price can be offered under current production conditions and related processes. For this reason, it is necessary to evaluate both the price acceptability from the customer's perspective and the ability of the price to cover all of the supplier's costs while ensuring at least a minimum level of profit (Čechová, 2011). Pricing policy is one of the most important areas of enterprise management. It directly affects business success and survival in a competitive environment.

Price setting and pricing decisions are typically made at the top management level. The quality of price-related decisions depends on the availability, timeliness, and relevance of information from other controlling functions.

In pricing decisions, it is necessary to obtain information about both the customer's willingness to pay and the supplier's cost structure. The market price represents the maximum threshold that customers are willing to pay for a product or service. Determining this price is the responsibility of other controlling departments, especially marketing, based on market research and consumer behavior.

Král et al. (2019) state that the key pricing criterion is the relationship between the quantity of products sold and the degree of capacity utilization. When these factors are aligned, prices stabilize and approach the equilibrium price—meaning customers are interested in the offered products, the price covers the costs, and there is neither a surplus nor a shortage. A high price enables higher profits or the ability to cover increased costs but limits demand. This results in market surplus and price reduction. Conversely, a low price stimulates demand but discourages supply. Market shortages then push the price upward.

The influence of competition on pricing is reflected in the level of interdependence among competitors (Fibírová, 2003). The closer the situation is to a monopoly, the greater the seller's ability to influence prices.

An important tool for internal pricing is the transfer price used for valuing outputs between departments. This price is a key instrument of responsibility-based management. Its main purpose is to coordinate internal relationships in a way that supports the overall objectives of the company. Transfer prices should motivate better decision-making, serve as a performance measure for departments, and reflect the authority and responsibility of internal units.

From Practice: Pricing Decision under Capacity Constraints
A precision tools manufacturer faced a tough decision: a key client requested a large custom order at a reduced price. The company had limited short-term capacity and ongoing long-term contracts.

Key dilemma: Should they accept the order and at what price?

Approach:

Full cost per unit: €15.80 (including fixed costs)
Variable cost per unit: €9.50
Offered price: €11.00
The management used contribution margin analysis and discovered that:
Even at €11.00, the contribution margin per unit was positive (€1.50).
The production would utilize idle capacity during night shifts.
Fixed costs were already covered by other orders.

Decision:

The company accepted the order using variable costing principles, focusing on contribution margin. They also used this opportunity to negotiate long-term cooperation with the client.

Outcome:

The company was able to generate additional profit by accepting a special order during a period of low demand, which allowed it to make use of otherwise idle production capacity. This decision did not cause any disruption to existing contracts, ensuring that regular customer commitments continued to be met without compromise. As a result of fulfilling the special request, the company also strengthened its relationship with the client, which may enhance trust and lead to greater pricing flexibility or negotiation power in the future.

2.8.4 Variance Analysis

JOne of the core objectives of operational controlling is to determine the expected value of performance indicators, compare them with their actual results, and analyze the differences. This process is applied both in cost calculations and budgeting. Variance analysis compares predetermined values, known as standards, with actual results (Drury, 2023). Its main contribution lies in measuring the effects of factors that influence the actual profit development in comparison to its expected value.

The system of variance-based management consists of the following steps (Fibírová et al., 2020):

1. Setting Standards

   A standard represents a predetermined value of cost, price, profit, or a resource expressed per unit of output. The first step is to clearly define the performance unit to which standards will apply.

   Next, primary standards are determined—these relate directly to the performance unit, such as selling price, material consumption, energy usage, or labor. These consumption standards are then priced using standard prices, resulting in standard unit costs and variable overhead standards.

   In addition, the standard total output volume for a given period is determined, serving as the basis for calculating standard fixed costs per unit, allowing the determination of the standard profit.

   In cases of non-homogeneous production—where financial indicators are influenced by the product mix—a standard product mix is also defined, reflecting the anticipated ratio in which various products will be produced.
2. Recording Actual Results
3. Identifying Variances Between Standard and Actual Values

   A variance is the difference between the standard and actual value of a specific variable. A positive variance occurs when actual costs are lower than standard or actual revenues are higher than standard. A negative variance occurs when actual costs exceed standard or actual revenues fall below standard.

   Variance identification can take place after an activity is completed or a period ends, or it can be conducted continuously.

   The downside of post-period variance identification is that it does not allow for immediate corrective actions, and the exact causes and responsibilities may be harder to trace.

   Ongoing variance tracking, on the other hand, allows immediate identification of variances, root cause analysis, accountability assignment, and swift corrective action.
4. Variance Analysis

   The goal is to determine the causes behind deviations between standard and actual profit levels and to assign responsibility. The depth of the analysis depends on the target audience and the purpose of the evaluation. The company must define internal rules and methods for variance detection.
5. Corrective Actions

   The most frequently monitored variances include variance in variable costs, variance in fixed costs, variance in selling prices, variance in output volume, input structure variance, output mix variance (caused by changes in the assortment of sold products).

According to Lazar (2012), variances can be categorized as follows Table 2.4.

Table 2.4 Type of variances

Type of variance	Costs (inputs)	Revenues (outputs)
Quantitative	Change in quantity of material or labor consumed	Change in volume of outputs
Qualitative	Change in material prices or wage rates	Change in sales prices of outputs
Structural	Change in structure of material types or labor types	Change in structure or mix of output types

Source Lazar (2012)

From Practice: Variance Analysis and Cost Control
A food processing company implemented standard costing for a popular product—a bottled fruit drink. The standard unit cost was based on:
Standard materials: €0.60
Standard labor: €0.30
Standard overhead: €0.25
Total standard cost per unit: €1.15
After a quarter, actual costs per unit were:

Materials: €0.67
Labor: €0.28
Overhead: €0.30
Total actual cost per unit: €1.25

Variance Analysis Results:

Material price variance: €0.07 unfavorable → supplier cost increased
Labor efficiency variance: €0.02 favorable → better team performance
Overhead spending variance: €0.05 unfavorable → energy cost spikes

Corrective Actions:

Corrective actions were taken to address the unfavorable cost variances. The company negotiated a bulk purchase contract for materials, which helped to secure more stable and favorable pricing. To address labor inefficiencies, it invested in staff training programs aimed at improving productivity. Additionally, an energy efficiency audit was launched to identify and reduce excessive energy consumption.

Impact:

As a result of these measures, material costs stabilized in the following quarter. Monthly cost variance reports were introduced as a regular feature of management meetings, enhancing transparency and enabling more informed decision-making. Furthermore, there was a renewed emphasis across all cost centers on controlling the costs that they could directly influence.

2.8.5 Break-Even Analysis

The division of costs into variable and fixed costs is crucial not only for cost calculation and profit management but also enables decision-making regarding various operational alternatives, analyzing the impact of changes in volume and product mix on profit, and optimizing the product structure. For easier analysis, a linear model of cost and revenue development is often used. This model represents a target that should be achieved. The assumptions of the linear model include a defined output and its predetermined structure, constant price, constant unit variable costs, total fixed costs, the ability to separate costs into variable and fixed components, and stable technology and labor productivity.

Management needs to know how many units of output must be sold to achieve the desired profit. Likewise, they must know how many units need to be sold to avoid a loss. This is determined using break-even analysis, where the break-even point is defined as the volume of output sold at which total revenues equal total costs (McWatters et al., 2008).

Break-even analysis allows the company to identify the critical point. Based on this analysis, the company can determine how changes in sales volume, selling prices, or costs affect profit. This analysis requires separate tracking of fixed and variable costs (Vollmuth, 2004). Break-even analysis also helps identify the margin of safety, which indicates how much sales can decline before reaching the break-even sales level (i.e., where revenues equal total costs), and the safety ratio, which shows by what percentage sales can drop before the company incurs a loss.

The Margin of Safety is a financial metric used in break-even analysis to measure how much sales can decrease before a business starts to incur losses. It represents the difference between the actual (or projected) sales and the break-even sales level.

This concept is crucial for assessing the risk of operations. A higher margin of safety indicates a greater buffer against unexpected drops in sales, while a lower margin suggests that even a small decline in revenue could push the company into a loss.

Why It Matters:

- Helps managers understand how much sales volume can decline before losses occur.
- Provides insight into operational risk and financial health.
- Useful in decision-making, especially during pricing, budgeting, and cost management.

The Margin of Safety Ratio expresses this buffer as a percentage of actual sales. It shows what proportion of the current sales volume can be lost before the break-even point is reached (Fig. 2.1).

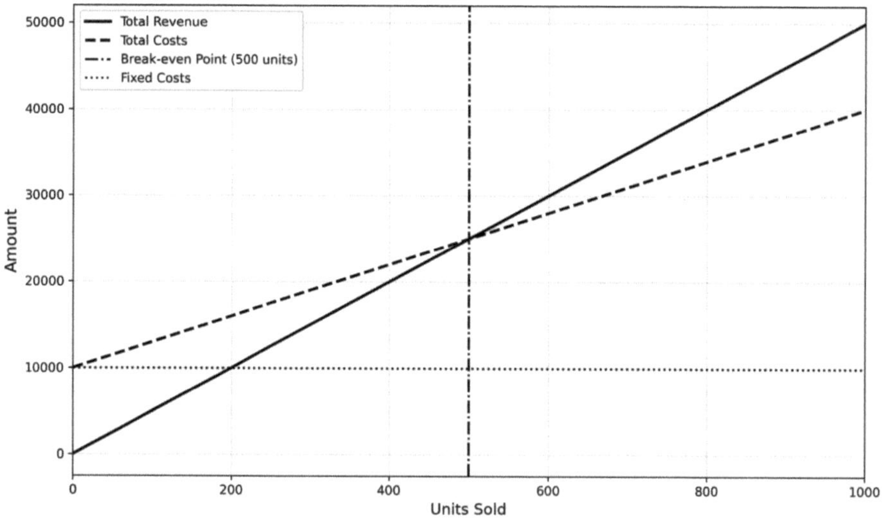

Fig. 2.1 Break-even analysis. *Source* Own processing

Formulas

$$\text{Break} - \text{even units} = \text{Fixed Costs} \div (\text{Price per Unit} - \text{Variable Cost per Unit})$$

$$\text{Margin of Safety (units)} = \text{Actual Sales - Break - even Sales}$$

$$\text{Margin of Safety (€)} = \text{Margin of Safety (units)} \times \text{Selling Price per Unit}$$

$$\text{Margin of Safety Ratio} = \text{Margin of Safety (units)} \div \text{Actual Sales (units)}$$

From Practice: Break-even Point Example + Margin of Safety

Scenario:

A company produces a single product.
Fixed Costs = € 10,000
Variable Costs per unit = € 30
Selling Price per unit = € 50
Actual Sales Volume = 700 units

To determine how many units must be sold to cover all costs:

Break-even Point Calculation:

$$\text{Break} - \text{even units} = \text{Fixed Costs} \div (\text{Price per Unit} - \text{Variable Cost per Unit})$$

$$= 10000 \div (50\text{—}30) = 500 \text{ units}$$

Margin of Safety Calculation:

$$\text{Margin of Safety (units)} = 700 - 500 = 200\,\text{units}$$

$$\text{Margin of Safety (€)} = 200 \times 50 = €10,000$$

Margin of Safety Ratio:

$$\text{Margin of Safety Ratio} = 200 \div 700 = 0.286 = 28.6\%$$

Interpretation:

At 500 units sold, the company neither makes a profit nor a loss. Selling more than 500 units generates profit, while selling fewer results in a loss.

The Margin of Safety is 200 units or € 10,000—meaning this is how much sales can drop before the company incurs a loss.

The Margin of Safety Ratio is 28.6%, which means revenues could decrease by almost one-third before the company hits the break-even point.

2.8.6 Other Operational Controlling Tools

The previously discussed methods represent the most well-known and most frequently used tools of operational controlling. However, there are several other, less common methods that are used only by some businesses. These include:

- ABC Analysis—The principle of this method lies in the idea that a small portion of the total volume can generate a disproportionately large value. This method can be applied to inventories, suppliers, customers, etc. Items are classified into three categories: A, B, and C. Class A represents 5% of items that generate 75% of the value; class B includes 20% of items that contribute 20% of the value; and class C represents 75% of items that only account for 5% of the value. Companies should focus on class A items, as they can have a significant impact on achieving business goals (Mikovcová, 2007).

- XYZ Analysis—This method is used in procurement, particularly for materials, based on consumption patterns. Material is classified as type X, Y, or Z. Type X materials have steady and predictable consumption; type Y materials show variability with a discernible trend; and type Z materials have irregular consumption. The tool helps in deciding the purchasing intervals for each type: type X is purchased in sync with production, type Y is purchased for inventory, and type Z is purchased on a case-by-case basis (Vollmuth, 2004).
- Value Analysis—This tool is used in managing current assets during various production phases. The main goal is to reduce the cost of individual products while ensuring their required functionality at the lowest possible cost—without compromising quality or reliability. The task is to find the optimal balance between cost and utility (Mikovcová, 2007).
- Sales Area Analysis—The objective is to identify differences in margins across various sales regions of the company. Weaker sales areas are compared with the strongest ones, and deviations are analyzed in terms of their underlying causes (e.g., reasons for lower turnover, higher sales costs, or higher storage expenses) (Vollmuth, 2004).

Other tools include:

- Order Volume Analysis
- Optimal Production Batch Size Calculation
- Order Quantity Optimization
- Sales Area Profitability Analysis
- Commission Analysis.

2.8.7 Operational Controlling Tools Summary

Operational controlling is a set of tools that help businesses effectively manage their day-to-day operations. It focuses primarily on costs, revenues, profitability, and process optimization within a shorter time frame, typically from several months to three years.

One of the core tools is cost calculation, which determines how much it costs to produce a specific product or service. These calculations are essential for planning, pricing, and monitoring efficiency. Closely related are various cost allocation methods, which ensure fair and accurate distribution of costs across different outputs or departments.

Budgeting is another important element; it involves preparing plans that define financial goals and expected developments in costs and revenues. Budgets help align the interests of different departments, serve as control mechanisms, and motivate performance improvement.

Operational controlling also supports pricing decisions, which consider not only internal costs but also market conditions, competition, and intra-company transactions. Setting appropriate prices is crucial for a company's competitiveness and profitability.

Another essential tool is variance analysis, which compares actual performance to planned figures and helps identify the causes of deviations. This allows businesses to respond more quickly and implement corrective measures.

Break-even analysis is a specific tool that identifies the sales volume at which the company begins to generate profit. It offers insight into how revenues, costs, and profit are interrelated.

In addition to these key instruments, there are other methods such as ABC and XYZ analysis, value analysis, or sales area and order analysis, which provide deeper insights into cost structures and help uncover opportunities for improvement.

Overall, operational controlling tools are vital for managing business performance, ensuring efficiency, and maintaining control over key financial indicators.

2.9 Strategic Management Tools in Controlling

Every company should choose appropriate strategic tools for its management processes, as well as define the criteria by which it will measure strategic performance. These tools and criteria must align with the company's long-term goals and vision to ensure that strategic objectives are met effectively.

Historically, the general objective of a business was to achieve maximum profit. In today's environment, however, businesses tend to focus more on maximizing the return on invested capital. This is typically measured using profitability indicators such as Return on Investment (ROI) or Economic Value Added (EVA). Some organizations also prioritize the maximization of the market value of the business. While these objectives may vary in terminology and scope, they all share a common foundation—the aim to maximize the value-based outcomes of the enterprise.

According to Preissler (2020), strategic controlling methods can be divided into two fundamental categories: qualitative methods and quantitative methods.

Qualitative methods focus on identifying the current factors influencing business performance, understanding their causes, and estimating their potential impacts. These methods are often used in the initial stage of strategic analysis and rely heavily on experience, intuition, and expert judgment. They include tools such as the SWOT analysis (Strengths, Weaknesses, Opportunities, Threats), PEST analysis (Political, Economic, Social, and Technological factors), the Delphi method, and scenario planning techniques. These approaches help organizations assess their external and internal environments and identify strategic risks and opportunities.

Quantitative methods, on the other hand, aim to assign measurable, numerical value to the insights derived from qualitative analysis. They are often used to validate assumptions and to support decision-making with data-based evidence. These methods may include time-series analysis, causal models, and predictive modeling techniques. By using statistical and econometric tools, organizations can simulate various strategic scenarios, forecast future developments, and evaluate the financial impact of different strategic choices.

The integration of both qualitative and quantitative methods allows for a more comprehensive approach to strategic controlling. While qualitative tools provide depth and context, quantitative tools offer precision and objectivity. When used together, they enable decision-makers to navigate complex strategic environments with a balanced perspective.

2.9.1 PEST Analysis

PEST analysis, also known as macro-environmental analysis, is a strategic tool used to identify and evaluate the external factors that can significantly influence the current and future operations of an organization. It provides a structured framework for analyzing the broader environment in which a business operates, helping decision-makers to anticipate potential threats and opportunities that may arise beyond the internal scope of the company.

The term "PEST" is an acronym that stands for Political, Economic, Social, and Technological factors. These four categories represent the key domains of influence that shape the macro-environment. In some extended versions of the analysis, legal and environmental aspects are also included, leading to variations such as PESTLE or STEEPLE analysis. Regardless of the format, the core objective remains the same: to enable organizations to align their strategic planning with external realities.

The main purpose of PEST analysis is to recognize critical macro-level factors and stakeholder influences that could impact the future performance and viability of the business. Based on the findings of the analysis, companies can formulate appropriate strategies to mitigate risks, leverage opportunities, and integrate these considerations into their operational and strategic planning.

The following components are typically examined during a PEST analysis:

- Political and legal factors—These include the political stability of the country or region, the structure and policies of the government, the influence of powerful political groups related to the industry, regulatory frameworks, tax policies, labor laws, trade restrictions, and overall legal environment. These factors can significantly affect how a company operates and how favorable the business climate is.
- Economic factors—This includes the overall economic climate, such as the stage of the economic cycle (growth, recession), inflation rates, interest rates, exchange rates, employment levels, disposable income of consumers, fiscal and monetary policy measures, and broader economic trends that influence purchasing power and capital availability.
- Social and cultural factors—These relate to the demographic profile of the population, lifestyle trends, education levels, cultural attitudes, consumer preferences,

social norms, and population growth rates. Understanding these factors is vital for businesses aiming to align their products, services, and communication strategies with societal expectations.

- Technological factors—This encompasses the pace of technological innovation, the availability and adoption of new technologies within the industry, levels of investment in research and development, automation trends, and the emergence of disruptive technologies. These factors can shape product development, operational efficiency, and competitiveness.

By conducting a thorough PEST analysis, companies gain valuable insight into the external forces that are beyond their direct control but which must be taken into account for successful long-term planning. The analysis helps organizations to proactively adapt their strategies, better prepare for uncertainties, and strengthen their ability to remain competitive in a dynamic environment (Mikovcová, 2007).

From Practice: PEST Analysis in the Automotive Industry Expansion
A European automotive supplier considering expansion into Southeast Asia conducted a comprehensive PEST analysis as part of its strategic planning process. The goal was to assess potential risks and opportunities in the target market before committing to major investments in manufacturing and distribution.

Political and Legal Factors:

The analysis revealed that the target country offered significant incentives for foreign investors in the automotive sector, including tax holidays and reduced import duties on machinery. However, the political climate was characterized by recent changes in leadership and uncertainty around future trade agreements. As a result, the company decided to partner with a local firm to mitigate potential regulatory and compliance risks.

Economic Factors:

The region showed strong GDP growth, a rising middle class, and increasing demand for vehicles. However, exchange rate volatility and inflationary trends posed risks to cost stability. The company built currency fluctuation buffers into its financial models and adopted a phased investment plan to manage exposure.

Social and Cultural Factors:

Consumer preferences in the region leaned heavily toward compact and fuel-efficient vehicles. The company adjusted its product portfolio, emphasizing smaller models with modern infotainment systems, and redesigned its marketing strategy to align with local values, such as community and environmental responsibility.

Technological Factors:

While the country had growing infrastructure and 4G connectivity, it lagged behind in EV (electric vehicle) readiness. However, the government had recently announced a national plan to promote green mobility. The company included EV development in its long-term roadmap, positioning itself for future growth aligned with technological progress in the region.

Outcome:

Thanks to the PEST analysis, the company was able to enter the market with a well-informed strategy, avoiding several pitfalls encountered by competitors. The structured approach to macro-environmental analysis allowed the company to align its expansion plan with external realities and increase its chances of sustainable success.

2.9.2 SWOT Analysis

The SWOT analysis is a fundamental strategic tool based on identifying and combining a company's Strengths, Weaknesses, Opportunities, and Threats. It provides a structured approach to assess internal capabilities and external environmental factors that influence the organization's strategic positioning and future development.

The main purpose of the SWOT analysis is to utilize strengths to minimize threats and to capitalize on opportunities. Conversely, weaknesses should be addressed or mitigated by leveraging available opportunities. Strengths and weaknesses typically include internal factors such as cost structure, product quality, pricing, innovation capacity, R&D performance, management style, and production portfolio. On the other hand, opportunities and threats are external in nature and may include factors like market trends, regulatory changes, competitive dynamics, and technological developments.

An important role of SWOT analysis is also the quantification of the impact of individual threats and opportunities, which allows for more informed decision-making and prioritization of strategic initiatives.

The SWOT matrix is often presented in a 2×2 format, dividing internal and external factors into four quadrants (Scheme 2.5).

According to Konečný and Režňáková (2005), the SWOT analysis is carried out in six key steps. The first two focus on reviewing past performance, while the remaining four steps deal with the future potential of the enterprise:

1. Collecting a summary of the company's past successes and failures.
   This step involves gathering historical data on operational, financial, and strategic outcomes.
2. Team discussion and root cause analysis of these successes and failures.
   A team of experts, often from various departments, evaluates the underlying factors contributing to past results.
3. Individual formulation of internal strengths and weaknesses by each team member.

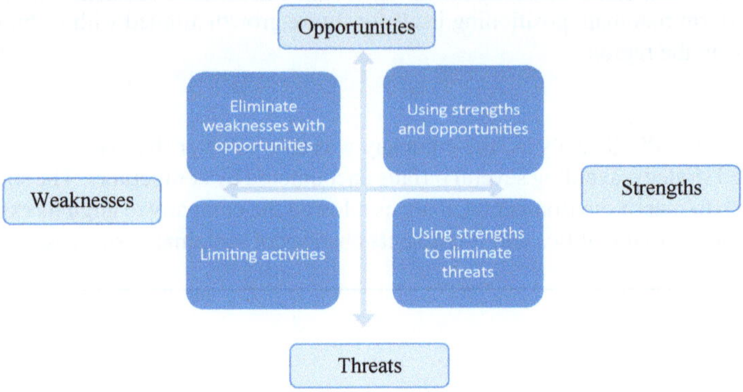

Scheme 2.5 SWOT analysis. *Source* Author's own elaboration

These can range from internal resources and capabilities to structural deficiencies or inefficiencies.

4. Identification of future external opportunities and threats, with a strong focus on the company's business environment.

   This step involves analyzing market, industry, regulatory, and technological changes that could impact the organization.
5. Evaluation of internal factors for the future, using a standardized scoring system, such as a ten-point scale, to assess their significance and strategic weight.
6. Presentation of SWOT results in a concise and communicable format.

   The final matrix should inform strategic decision-making, serving as a basis for setting priorities and aligning resources.

SWOT analysis is often used in conjunction with other strategic tools like PEST analysis, Porter's Five Forces, or scenario planning, to provide a comprehensive view of both internal capabilities and external challenges.

When applied rigorously, SWOT becomes not just a descriptive method but a diagnostic and predictive instrument that supports long-term value creation and sustainable competitive advantage.

From Practice: SWOT Analysis in a Mid-Sized Manufacturing Company

A mid-sized Czech manufacturing company specializing in precision mechanical components faced stagnating growth and increasing pressure from international competitors. In response, the company's management initiated a strategic planning process using a structured SWOT analysis.

Step 1: Internal Analysis—Strengths and Weaknesses

Through team workshops and performance reviews, the company identified several key strengths, including:

- High product quality with a defect rate below 1%.

- Long-standing relationships with key clients in the automotive industry.
- Strong in-house engineering and R&D capabilities.

On the other hand, the team acknowledged significant weaknesses:

- Limited digital marketing and sales capabilities.
- Dependence on a small number of clients for over 60% of revenue.
- Outdated ERP systems causing inefficiencies in inventory and planning.

Step 2: External Analysis—Opportunities and Threats

The team analyzed external trends and gathered insights from industry reports and customer feedback, identifying the following opportunities:

- Growing demand for customized components in e-mobility.
- Availability of EU subsidies for digital transformation.
- Potential partnerships with international distributors.

However, several threats were also recognized:

- Increasing price competition from Asian manufacturers.
- Rising raw material costs and supply chain disruptions.
- New environmental regulations requiring investment in cleaner technologies.

Step 3: Strategic Implications

Using the SWOT matrix, the management team formulated strategic options:

- SO strategy: Leverage R&D capabilities (strength) to develop new e-mobility components (opportunity).
- WO strategy: Use available subsidies (opportunity) to upgrade ERP systems and digitalize sales (weakness).
- ST strategy: Differentiate through quality and reliability (strength) to reduce the impact of cheaper competitors (threat).
- WT strategy: Diversify client portfolio (addressing weakness) to reduce risk exposure from raw material price volatility (threat).

Outcome:

The company developed a two-year strategic roadmap based on this analysis, focusing on digital transformation, product innovation, and market diversification. Within 18 months, they secured two new international clients, launched a new product line for the EV sector, and received partial funding for IT upgrades. Management reported increased internal alignment and improved risk awareness across departments.

2.9.3 BCG Matrix

In the 1970s, the consulting firm Boston Consulting Group developed the BCG matrix with the aim of optimizing the product portfolio for strategic management of corporate cash flows. The primary goal of portfolio analysis is to identify market areas with expected positive development where the company can apply its competitive advantage. According to Šoljaková (2009), the BCG matrix evaluates each product based on two key indicators:

- Relative market share, expressed as the ratio between the company's market share and that of its largest competitor,
- Market growth rate, measured as the annual growth rate of the market.

By combining these two indicators, the matrix estimates the contribution or generated cash flow of each product. This classification allows businesses to group their products into four categories (as shown in the accompanying chart):

1. Cash Cows—Products with low market growth but high market share that generate steady and substantial cash flow. These products often finance other areas of the portfolio. The focus here is on cost management and operational efficiency.
2. Stars—Products with high growth and high market share. Although they require significant investment, they represent the future of the company's profitability and competitive position. The strategic objective is to sustain or grow their market share while the market is expanding.
3. Dogs—Products with both low market growth and low market share. They usually produce minimal returns and maintaining them can be costly. Businesses should consider phasing them out or repositioning them.
4. Question Marks—Products in high-growth markets with low market share. These require strategic decisions: whether to invest and attempt to convert them into Stars or to divest. They are risky but may have substantial potential (Scheme 2.6).

The BCG matrix is also a valuable tool for resource allocation—for example, shifting investments from Dogs to high-potential Question Marks or Stars. However, while it offers a clear and visual framework, it also has limitations. Its key drawbacks include a static nature, focus on only two variables, and failure to account for other

Scheme 2.6 BCG matrix. *Source* Own processing

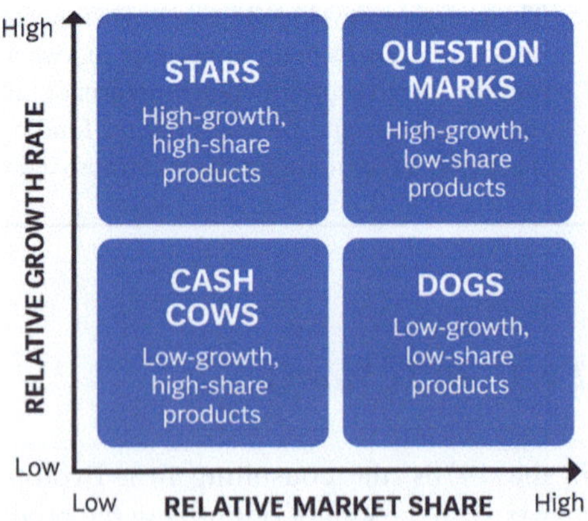

strategic factors such as product synergies, customer loyalty, market entry barriers, or operational risks.

Today, the BCG matrix is often supplemented or replaced by more advanced approaches such as Product Lifecycle Costing, Economic Value Added (EVA), or the GE/McKinsey Matrix, which provide a more multidimensional and comprehensive assessment of strategic performance across the portfolio.

From Practice: BCG Matrix in a Consumer Electronics Company
A European consumer electronics manufacturer decided to revise its product portfolio using the BCG Matrix to optimize investment decisions and focus resources more effectively. The company operated in segments including home entertainment systems, smartwatches, tablets, and wireless headphones.

Analysis and Classification:

- Cash Cows

  The company's home entertainment systems had a large market share in a mature market. Although the market growth was minimal, the segment generated stable and high cash flows. These products required only modest investment for maintenance and marketing. The management decided to "milk" this segment by maintaining its market presence while reallocating excess cash flow to more promising segments.
- Stars

  Wireless headphones, driven by the growing trend of remote work and fitness tracking, showed high market growth and strong company market share. The company heavily invested in R&D and branding to maintain its position and eventually transition this segment into future cash cows.
- Question Marks

  Smartwatches were gaining popularity globally, but the company had a relatively low market share in this competitive space. Management was faced with a decision: invest heavily in product development and marketing to try to become a significant player—or exit the segment. After market research and pilot campaigns, they decided to invest selectively in niche smartwatch features (e.g., elderly health monitoring), hoping to move this category into the Star quadrant.
- Dogs

  The tablet division had been declining due to intense competition and decreasing market interest. It had a low market share in a stagnant market. The decision was made to gradually phase out this product line and shift production capacity to wireless accessories.

Outcome:

The BCG Matrix helped the company identify underperforming segments, allocate resources based on future potential, and improve profitability. Within two years, they saw a 15% increase in return on capital employed (ROCE) and improved strategic focus across all departments.

2.9.4 Porter's Five Forces Model

Porter's Five Forces model, developed by Michael E. Porter in 1979, is one of the most recognized and widely used tools for analyzing the competitive environment of an industry. It is primarily used to assess industry attractiveness and profit potential. The model helps businesses understand the forces shaping competitive pressure and affecting their ability to generate profits. Its main purpose is to provide a strategic decision-making framework, whether entering a new market, developing new products, or revising a business model.

The model is based on the idea that the intensity of competition in an industry is not driven solely by existing competitors, but by five distinct forces that together shape the overall profitability of the market. If these forces are strong, the competitive environment becomes less attractive, putting pressure on prices, margins, and long-term profitability.

The Five Competitive Forces according to Porter:

1. Threat of Substitutes

   Customers may switch to alternative products or services that fulfill the same need more efficiently, cheaply, or conveniently. The greater the availability of substitutes, the higher the competitive pressure. For example, in certain contexts, high-speed rail can substitute air travel.
2. Bargaining Power of Suppliers

   Powerful suppliers can influence the price, quality, and availability of inputs, directly impacting a company's cost structure. This power increases when there are few suppliers, when inputs are unique, or when switching suppliers is costly or difficult.
3. Bargaining Power of Buyers (Customers)

   Buyers can exert pressure to lower prices, improve quality, or demand better service. Their power is greater when they have many alternatives, or when they purchase in large volumes. Companies try to reduce this power through brand loyalty, customization, or value-added services.
4. Threat of New Entrants

   New competitors entering the market can disrupt the status quo, particularly if they bring innovation, lower prices, or strong brand recognition. Entry barriers such as high initial investments, regulatory constraints, customer loyalty, or proprietary technology can mitigate this threat.
5. Rivalry Among Existing Competitors

   The intensity of competition depends on the number of players, industry growth rate, cost structures, and product differentiation. Higher rivalry often leads to price wars, increased marketing efforts, and accelerated innovation.

Businesses should use the Five Forces model not only when considering entry into a new industry but also to evaluate their current market position. It is a valuable strategic tool for identifying threats, understanding the dynamics of the industry, and uncovering opportunities to improve competitiveness Preissler (2020).

From Practice: Applying Porter's Five Forces in the Retail Sector
A mid-sized retail company specializing in consumer electronics used Porter's Five Forces model to evaluate the attractiveness of entering a new regional market. The management team systematically analyzed all five forces:

- Threat of Substitutes: The analysis revealed a growing trend of customers purchasing electronics online rather than in physical stores. This insight prompted the company to strengthen its e-commerce platform and integrate online and offline sales strategies to reduce the risk of substitution.
- Bargaining Power of Suppliers: Because the company sourced products from well-known global brands, it initially faced limited bargaining power. However, by negotiating bulk purchase agreements and diversifying its supplier base, the retailer improved its terms of delivery and reduced input costs.
- Bargaining Power of Buyers: The study showed that customers in the new region were highly price-sensitive and regularly compared offers online. As a result, the retailer introduced loyalty programs, extended warranties, and in-store services (e.g., installation) to create added value and reduce direct price competition.
- Threat of New Entrants: Although the market had potential for growth, entry barriers were relatively low. The company decided to invest in brand visibility and secure prime store locations before competitors could enter.
- Rivalry Among Existing Competitors: The analysis confirmed intense rivalry among established players, resulting in aggressive discounting. Instead of engaging in a price war, the retailer chose to differentiate through customer service quality and exclusive product bundles.

Outcome:

By using Porter's Five Forces model, the retailer identified not only risks but also opportunities to strengthen its market position before entry. The company's proactive strategy (combining e-commerce, loyalty programs, supplier diversification, and service differentiation) allowed it to achieve profitability within 18 months and establish itself as a recognized competitor in the new region.

2.9.5 *Target Costing*

Target costing is a strategic cost management method that has gained particular prominence in Japan and has also been adopted by select innovative firms in Europe and the United States; especially those operating in the technology, automotive, and engineering sectors. This approach emphasizes market orientation and customer value as the basis for cost planning and product development, rather than relying solely on traditional cost-plus pricing.

Unlike conventional costing methods that begin with cost estimation and then determine the selling price by adding a markup, target costing reverses this logic. It starts from the market: companies conduct detailed market research to understand customer needs, expectations, and the price customers are willing to pay for a specific product or service. This price becomes the target price—a realistic market-driven figure based on competitive analysis and customer value perception.

From this target price, a target profit margin is subtracted. This is not arbitrary but is usually derived from the company's strategic financial objectives, such as the required return on investment (ROI), return on capital employed (ROCE), or value creation goals like EVA (Economic Value Added). The result of this subtraction is the target cost—the maximum allowable cost to ensure the company remains competitive and profitable.

Target Costing Process (Popesko, 2009; Šoljaková, 2009):

1. Determine the Target Price

   The first step involves identifying a realistic price point based on customer expectations, market demand, and competitor pricing. This price should reflect not only the product's technical features and quality but also its perceived value throughout its life cycle. In many industries, pricing is influenced by substitute products and innovations, so the target price must also take these dynamics into account.The intensity of competition depends on the number of players, industry growth rate, cost structures, and product differentiation. Higher rivalry often leads to price wars, increased marketing efforts, and accelerated innovation.
2. Set the Target Profit Margin

   Next, companies define the required margin based on strategic financial goals. The profit margin should reflect the opportunity cost of capital and should be attractive enough to justify the investment in development, production, and marketing. For example, a firm might aim for a 15% profit margin based on its corporate strategy.The intensity of competition depends on the number of players, industry growth rate, cost structures, and product differentiation. Higher rivalry often leads to price wars, increased marketing efforts, and accelerated innovation.
3. Calculate the Target Cost

   The target cost is then derived by subtracting the target profit from the target price. This figure represents the cost ceiling—the maximum permissible cost that can be allocated to the product while still achieving the desired profit level.The intensity of competition depends on the number of players, industry growth rate, cost structures, and product differentiation. Higher rivalry often leads to price wars, increased marketing efforts, and accelerated innovation.

   $$\text{Target Cost} = \text{Target Price} - \text{Target Profit}$$

4. Compare Target Cost with Estimated (Projected) Cost

   At this point, the company compares the target cost with the estimated cost (or projected cost) of the product, as calculated through preliminary design and development assessments. If the projected cost exceeds the target cost, the product is not economically viable in its current form.
5. Cost Reduction through Value Engineering

If the target cost is not initially met, cross-functional teams are involved in value engineering and design-to-cost activities. These might include:

- Redesigning components
- Simplifying production processes
- Re-evaluating material selection
- Outsourcing non-core operations
- Revisiting supplier contracts
- Improving operational efficiency

These efforts are aimed at modifying the design and process before the product reaches the manufacturing stage to ensure cost targets are met without sacrificing quality or functionality.

6. Ongoing Cost Monitoring
   Even after the launch of a product, target costing encourages continuous cost monitoring and improvement, particularly in long product life cycles. The discipline becomes part of a broader lean management or kaizen framework.

Strategic Benefits of Target Costing

- Aligns product development with market realities and customer expectations.
- Helps avoid overengineering and unnecessary features that inflate costs.
- Promotes cross-functional collaboration early in the product development process.
- Ensures profitability is designed into the product from the outset.
- Enables companies to compete on both price and value.

Limitations

Despite its advantages, target costing may not be suitable for all industries—particularly those with highly volatile markets or where customization is a key differentiator. It also requires a mature organizational culture, robust communication across departments, and strong data analytics capabilities to be implemented effectively.

From Practice: Target Costing in the Automotive Industry—Toyota
Background:

Toyota, one of the pioneers in cost-efficient production systems, has long utilized the target costing approach as a core part of its product development process. A notable application occurred during the development of a new compact car model aimed at cost-sensitive markets such as Southeast Asia and South America.

Situation:

Toyota's strategic objective was to introduce a competitively priced car in the subcompact segment to strengthen its position in emerging markets. Through extensive market research and benchmarking, Toyota identified that the acceptable market price for the car would need to be around €10,000, including a minimal profit margin of 10%.

Target Cost Calculation:

- Target Price: €10,000
- Target Profit Margin: €1,000
- Target Cost: €9000

However, the initial cost estimate from engineering and procurement teams was €10,800, significantly exceeding the target cost by €1800.

Action Taken:

A cross-functional task force was assembled, including members from Product design, Engineering, Procurement, Marketing, Finance.

The team undertook a value engineering process that involved:

- Design simplification: The number of components in the dashboard was reduced by 40%.
- Material optimization: Use of high-strength lightweight steel instead of aluminum in non-structural parts.
- Supplier collaboration: Long-term contracts were negotiated with key parts suppliers to reduce per-unit cost.
- Platform sharing: Components were standardized with existing models to benefit from economies of scale.

Outcome:

After several iterations and detailed cost analysis, the redesigned vehicle met the target cost of €9000 without compromising quality or safety standards.

Strategic Impact:

- The vehicle was launched at the target price and quickly gained significant market share in targeted regions.
- The company maintained its desired profit margin.
- Lessons learned from this process were later applied to other global models, reinforcing Toyota's reputation for efficiency and value.

2.9.6 Product Life Cycle Costing (Lifecycle Costing)

Product life cycle costing is a strategic cost management tool that focuses on evaluating and managing the total costs, revenues, and profits associated with a product over its entire economic life cycle. This approach shares many similarities with target costing, but extends its application to cover all phases of a product's life—from initial research and development, through production and sale, to post-sale support and eventual market withdrawal.

The primary aim of life cycle costing is to provide a comprehensive view of a product's financial performance by accounting for all expenses and income related to the product throughout its life span. It is particularly useful in industries with high upfront investment costs and long product development cycles, such as automotive, aerospace, electronics, or pharmaceuticals.

According to Šoljaková (2009), life cycle costing can be expressed in two distinct forms depending on the purpose of the analysis:

- Costing by Partial Periods: This version breaks down the costs, revenues, and profits into individual time intervals, reflecting the forecasted financial development over the product's life. It allows for more granular insight into specific phases, such as the introduction period or decline.
- Costing Over the Entire Evaluation Period: This method calculates a weighted average of all expected costs, revenues, and profits over the entire life cycle. It is particularly suitable for long-term planning, profitability forecasting, and investment decisions.

The calculation of life cycle costs is based on several key assumptions and inputs:

- The expected length of the product's life cycle,
- Total sales volume over its lifetime,
- Anticipated price development,
- Projected evolution of product-related costs (Popesko, 2009).

The typical phases of a product's life cycle include:

1. Introduction Phase: Characterized by high risk, high costs, and low or slow-growing sales and turnover. Marketing, promotion, and development costs are significant in this phase. The strategic goal is usually to gain initial market share.
2. Growth Phase: Sales volume increases rapidly, economies of scale are achieved, and unit costs start to decrease. This phase offers an opportunity to improve profitability, establish brand presence, and optimize production.
3. Maturity Phase: Sales growth slows, and the product reaches its peak market penetration. Revenues and profits stabilize or peak. Maintaining market share often requires additional investments in marketing and product differentiation.
4. Decline Phase: Sales, turnover, profits, and cash flows begin to fall due to market saturation, emerging substitutes, or changing customer preferences. Strategic decisions must be made about whether to discontinue the product, find niche markets, or extend its lifecycle through innovation or cost reduction.

If the product moves into production, the forecasted life cycle cost plan is continuously monitored and compared with actual incurred costs. One of the key limitations of life cycle costing is that it provides limited opportunity for corrective action once production begins, especially if deviations are discovered too late. Costs already incurred become sunk costs. However, this analysis serves as a valuable learning tool for improving accuracy and cost control in the planning of future products.

Having access to life cycle costing data for multiple products also allows a company to create a multi-year budgeted income statement and cash flow forecast. By coordinating the timing of product life cycles, a business can offset loss-making periods of one product with profit-making phases of another, thus achieving more stable overall financial performance.

Moreover, life cycle costing supports strategic decisions about:

- The optimal time to launch or withdraw products from the market,
- Planning research and development investments,
- Managing capacity and resource allocation,
- Forecasting profitability and long-term value creation.

In conclusion, product life cycle costing is an essential instrument for comprehensive cost control and value management, especially in highly dynamic or innovation-driven industries. It shifts the focus from short-term cost control to long-term financial planning and strategic profitability.

From Practice: Life-Cycle Costing in the Automotive Industry

Company Context:

An established European car manufacturer was preparing to launch a new electric vehicle (EV). Management decided to use life-cycle costing (LCC) to evaluate the total financial impact of the product over its expected 10-year market life.

Planning Phase:

The LCC team began by estimating R&D costs, tooling expenses, and promotional budgets for the introduction phase. They also forecasted expected sales volume, average selling price, and unit production costs for each phase of the life cycle.

Estimated Life-Cycle Breakdown (EUR):
- Development & Launch Costs: €250 million
- Average unit cost over life cycle: €18,000
- Expected total units sold: 200,000
- Average selling price per unit: €28,000
- Marketing and support (total): €100 million
- Estimated gross profit over lifecycle: €1.650 million

Modeling:

Life cycle stage	Duration (years)	Revenue (€ mil.)	Cost (€ mil.)	Profit/loss (€ mil.)	note
1. Development and introduction	0–2	0	250	−250	Development, testing, investment in technology and production
2. Growth	3–5	1500	1100	400	Rapid sales growth, higher unit costs, high marketing expenses

(continued)

(continued)

Life cycle stage	Duration (years)	Revenue (€ mil.)	Cost (€ mil.)	Profit/loss (€ mil.)	note
3. Maturity	6–9	3500	2000	1500	Stable sales, decreased unit costs due to economies of scale
4. Decline	10–11	600	600	0	Demand drops, production ends, clearance sales
Total	0–11	5600	3950	1650	Gross profit before taxes and adjustments

Insight:

Although the vehicle was initially projected to generate low or negative margins during the introduction phase, the LCC approach justified the investment by showing significant profitability during the growth and maturity stages.

Additionally, the company planned overlapping product cycles to offset losses during the EV's early years with profits from mature models.

Lessons Learned:

- Without LCC, the high upfront development costs might have discouraged the project.
- The company gained better timing of investments and cash flow planning.
- They were also able to strategically plan future model releases based on the lifecycle curves of current models.

2.9.7 Just in Time (JIT) Method

The Just in Time (JIT) method is a strategic approach to production and inventory management that focuses on permanent and long-term cost reduction by minimizing the time required for individual processes and eliminating non-value-adding activities. The ultimate goal of JIT is to maximize efficiency, improve product quality, and reduce total costs by streamlining operations throughout the entire supply chain.

JIT is fundamentally about producing or acquiring only what is needed, when it is needed, and in the exact quantity needed. It aligns production schedules closely with actual customer demand, eliminating the need for excessive inventory and unnecessary stockpiling. The method is particularly effective in lean manufacturing environments and is widely used in sectors like automotive, electronics, and precision engineering.

Core Objectives of JIT:

- Reduce or eliminate wasteful activities that do not add value to the product or service (e.g., excessive transportation, overproduction, waiting times).
- Enhance workflow efficiency by synchronizing operations and ensuring materials flow smoothly through each stage of the production process.
- Improve productivity and responsiveness to market demands.
- Lower the total cost of ownership (TCO) through better resource utilization.

JIT can be applied in two main areas:

1. JIT Purchasing (Just in Time Purchasing):

   Involves ordering raw materials or components so they arrive precisely when needed in the production process.

   Helps avoid unnecessary capital being tied up in inventory and reduces the need for large storage facilities.
2. JIT Manufacturing (Just in Time Production):

   Focuses on producing goods only when there is customer demand, preventing the buildup of finished goods inventory.

   Encourages continuous improvement and flexible production systems.

Benefits of the JIT Approach:

- Reduced ordering and receiving costs: Smaller, more frequent orders reduce administrative costs and streamline supplier interactions.
- Lower inventory holding costs: Minimizes the need for warehousing, insurance, and storage space.
- Decreased risk associated with safety stock: Less reliance on buffer stock means fewer obsolete or expired items.
- Improved coordination between linked activities: Synchronizing production steps reduces downtime and bottlenecks between departments.
- Access to quantity discounts: Frequent but well-planned purchases can still take advantage of volume-based pricing or long-term supplier agreements.
- Capacity balancing in seasonal industries: JIT helps optimize resource usage during peak and off-peak demand periods by adjusting production accordingly.

Challenges and Requirements for Successful Implementation:

- While JIT offers many benefits, its successful implementation requires:
- Strong relationships with reliable suppliers, who can deliver on short notice with high consistency.
- Accurate demand forecasting to avoid stockouts or overproduction.
- A highly flexible production system capable of quickly adjusting to changes in order volumes or product specifications.
- Employee involvement and cross-training, since workforce flexibility is critical for adapting to process changes.
- Robust information systems to support real-time data sharing and inventory tracking.

From Practice: Implementation of JIT in an Automotive Supplier

Company Context:

A mid-sized Czech manufacturer producing components for the automotive industry. It faced several issues typical for traditional manufacturing systems:

- High inventory levels led to significant warehousing costs.
- Frequent delays between production steps due to misaligned scheduling.
- Overproduction of parts that were later not used, resulting in scrap and financial losses.
- Cash flow constraints caused by capital tied up in stock.

Steps Taken in JIT Implementation:

1. Supplier Coordination:
   The company renegotiated contracts with its three key suppliers to enable daily deliveries instead of weekly bulk shipments. This required real-time data sharing about component needs.

Results After 9 Months:

- Inventory reduction by 42%, freeing up €280,000 in working capital.
- Warehouse space reduced by 35%, allowing its partial conversion into an assembly line for a new product.
- On-time delivery rate improved from 89 to 98%.
- Production lead time decreased by 30%, increasing responsiveness to client changes.

Key Takeaways:

By implementing JIT, the company not only achieved cost savings, but also enhanced operational agility and improved customer satisfaction. While the transition required up-front investment in planning and staff training, the return on investment was reached within the first year.

2.9.8 Other Strategic Controlling Tools

The previously discussed methods represent the most well-known and commonly applied tools in strategic controlling. However, several additional methods, although used less frequently, can provide valuable insights and support long-term planning and strategic decision-making. These include:

Potential Analysis

Potential analysis focuses on evaluating and managing internal capabilities and opportunities that can be developed to ensure long-term competitiveness. A "potential" in this context is a measurable and manageable resource or capability. This analysis builds upon the outcomes of SWOT analysis (particularly internal strengths and weaknesses) and complements it with inputs from PEST analysis and industry analysis. The goal is to identify the key success factors for a company within its market environment.

Once the key success factors are determined, the organization compares its current performance to that of the leading competitors or market leaders. This benchmarking helps to identify competitive gaps and opportunities for strategic development. For example, if a market leader excels in digital customer experience and the subject company lacks in this area, the analysis can highlight digitalization as a key area for investment.

Potential analysis enables:

- Recognition of internal capabilities that are critical for future growth
- Prioritization of development initiatives
- Strategic alignment of resources

Strategic Balance

Strategic balance examines the dependencies between a company and its stakeholders, emphasizing the need to maintain a sustainable equilibrium. It differentiates between:

- Active dependencies: The degree to which stakeholders depend on the company
- Passive dependencies: The degree to which the company depends on stakeholders

To begin, a list of stakeholders is created (e.g., customers, suppliers, regulators, employees, investors), along with their expectations and demands. In parallel, the company's requirements from each stakeholder group are defined. The degree of dependency is quantified, typically on a scale from 0% (no dependency) to 100% (total dependency).

If passive dependencies significantly outweigh active ones, the company is considered vulnerable and may need to adjust its strategy. Maintaining strategic balance ensures that the company is resilient and retains bargaining power within its environment.

Strategic Gap Analysis

Strategic gap analysis identifies the difference between a company's desired future state (based on strategic goals) and its likely future state (assuming no major changes or strategic initiatives). This method highlights long-term deviations between planned and probable development paths.

- Desired development: A target state derived from strategic objectives
- Probable development: A projected state based on current trends and no new strategic actions

A strategic gap exists when there is a discrepancy between these two trajectories. The wider the gap, the more urgent the need for corrective measures such as new investments, market expansion, innovation, or organizational restructuring. Regular gap analysis ensures that the company remains proactive in achieving its goals and doesn't drift from its strategic path.

Scenario Planning

Scenario planning is a structured method for exploring and preparing for multiple future developments. It is especially valuable in volatile and uncertain business environments, where traditional forecasting may be insufficient.

The process begins with an analysis of the current situation and identification of the most influential external and internal factors. These may include technological advancements, regulatory changes, market behavior, competitive dynamics, and macroeconomic shifts.

Scenarios are then developed based on combinations of these factors, typically covering:

- Optimistic scenario: A best-case future with favorable conditions
- Pessimistic scenario: A worst-case future highlighting risks and downturns
- Neutral or trend-based scenario: The most likely development if current trends continue

Companies can then test their strategies against each scenario to assess robustness and flexibility. This promotes readiness and adaptability, helping management to make informed decisions under uncertainty.

These less commonly used tools of strategic controlling offer a deeper understanding of long-term influences and stakeholder dynamics. They complement traditional instruments like the BCG matrix or SWOT analysis by addressing strategic dependencies, potential capabilities, and uncertainty. Implementing these tools can greatly enhance a company's ability to formulate resilient strategies and maintain competitive advantage over time.

2.10 Controlling Reporting

Reporting is one of the most essential tools within the controlling system. Its main objective is to provide a comprehensive and structured information system that evaluates the performance of a company as a whole as well as its individual organizational units, in accordance with the requirements of management. Reports should be structured in a way that aligns with the decision-making needs of users at various management levels (Fibírová, 2003).

According to Eschenbach and Siller (2012), a high-quality reporting system must fulfill the following core functions:

- Document the current status and condition of the company in a reliable and traceable manner to serve as a basis for analysis.
- Identify and map all key value drivers that affect performance.
- Serve as an information backbone for planning, analysis, management, and regulation, thereby increasing the quality of managerial decision-making.
- Report both current and forecasted deviations from plans and targets.

- Present information in a clear, concise, and meaningful format that enables effective interpretation.
- Be tailored to the specific informational needs of each recipient to ensure relevance and usability.

An integral part of the reporting system includes Key Performance Indicators (KPIs), which serve as benchmarks for comparing actual performance with predetermined goals and targets. Depending on the organizational level, the structure and nature of these KPIs may vary:

- For relatively autonomous business units or divisions, synthetic financial indicators are commonly used, such as profitability ratios (e.g., Return on Investment, Return on Sales).
- For internal departments or cost centers, analytical indicators focusing on cost control and resource efficiency are more appropriate. These are often combined with physical (non-financial) indicators, such as output per employee or machine utilization rate.

Controlling reports are typically categorized by functional areas, including production, sales, human resources, marketing, R&D, and others. While the general framework of reporting follows a structured approach, the level of detail and report format may be adapted to suit the company's internal practices and specific needs. Flexibility in reporting allows for effective integration with the company's strategic and operational goals.

A key advantage of controlling-based reporting is its forward-looking nature. Unlike financial accounting, which is historically focused and governed by legal standards, controlling reports emphasize planning, forecasting, and variance analysis, which provide a basis for proactive management.

Reporting in controlling also supports transparency and accountability by tracking both planned vs. actual results and analyzing the causes of deviations. This enables corrective actions to be taken promptly and improves the responsiveness of the company to internal and external changes.

As part of this reporting system, special attention is given to performance reporting. This includes not only profit and cost reporting but also reporting on innovation, process efficiency, quality control, and customer satisfaction. Such multidimensional reporting allows for a holistic view of company performance.

The implementation of an effective reporting system requires the use of integrated IT systems (such as ERP and Business Intelligence platforms), which support automated data collection, real-time dashboards, and visualization tools that improve the clarity and accessibility of information.

In summary, controlling reporting is a dynamic management tool that links strategy with operations. It provides a vital bridge between planning, execution, and evaluation, helping companies steer toward long-term success by making informed, data-driven decisions.

Budgeted Balance Sheet Statement

The budgeted balance sheet is a crucial component of financial planning and controlling reporting. Unlike the income statement, which focuses on revenues and expenses over a period, the budgeted balance sheet offers a static snapshot of a company's projected financial position at a future date.

Purpose:

- Estimate the company's financial structure and health in the future.
- Assess solvency, liquidity, and financial stability.
- Support investment and financing decisions.
- Monitor the balance between assets and liabilities.
- Provide a basis for planning future funding needs.

Structure of the Budgeted Balance Sheet:

The budgeted balance sheet is structured similarly to a traditional financial balance sheet, divided into assets and liabilities & equity, but may use alternative valuations and incorporate economic perspectives.

1. Assets
    - Fixed Assets: Planned long-term investments, with values often based on market estimates or expected utility.
    - Current Assets:
        - Inventories (raw materials, work-in-progress, finished goods).
        - Receivables (based on projected sales and payment terms).
        - Cash and equivalents.
2. Liabilities and Equity
    - Equity: Includes share capital and retained earnings (including planned profits).
    - Liabilities:
        - Short-term liabilities (accounts payable, wages, taxes).
        - Long-term debt (bank loans, leases).
        - Provisions (for expected future expenses).

Controlling-Specific Features:

- Use of alternative valuation methods (e.g., market value, economic depreciation).
- Inclusion of intangible assets not typically shown in financial accounting.
- Cross-integration with other budgets (investment, working capital, cash flow).
- Allows for scenario analysis and forecasting under varying business assumptions.

From Practice: Implementation of a Budgeted Balance Sheet at TechNova Ltd.

Company Context:

TechNova Ltd., a medium-sized technology company specializing in industrial automation solutions, had experienced rapid growth in customer orders in recent years. To better manage this expansion, the company decided to introduce strategic and financial controlling tools, including the budgeted balance sheet, in order to gain a clearer view of its planned financial position in the coming fiscal year.

Objective:

To create a predictive overview of the company's assets, liabilities, and equity at the end of the upcoming fiscal year and to identify potential issues related to liquidity, debt levels, or investment needs.

Approach:

1. Estimation of Planned Revenues and Expenses:
   Based on planned contracts, market expansion into a new region, and projected R&D investments, multiple versions of the income statement, cash flow budget, and investment plan were prepared.

Results:

The budgeted balance sheet enabled the company to identify a working capital shortfall in advance, which could have otherwise led to serious cash flow issues.

Through scenario simulations, management decided to postpone part of the planned investments to reduce pressure on short-term liquidity.

The company introduced a new process for monthly updates of the budgeted balance sheet and cash flow forecasting as a tool for solvency and investment management.

Conclusion:

This study demonstrates that the budgeted balance sheet is not merely a theoretical tool but a practical and strategic foundation for making informed decisions about financing, investments, and risk management. Thanks to its implementation, TechNova achieved greater financial stability and the ability to manage growth without jeopardizing liquidity.

Budgeted Income Statement

A budgeted income statement is a planned profit and loss report that presents the expected financial performance of a business over a specific period, typically one year. It is a key output of financial planning within controlling and serves as an essential tool for managing business performance.

It is based on planned revenues (sales), planned costs (both variable and fixed), and the forecasted profit (or loss).

Structure of the Budgeted Income Statement

The budgeted income statement typically includes the following components:

1. Sales Revenue—estimated income from selling products or services.

2. Cost of Goods Sold (COGS)—direct material and labor costs.
3. Gross Profit—difference between sales and COGS.
4. Operating Expenses—fixed costs, overheads, depreciation, marketing, and administration.
5. Operating Profit (EBIT)—earnings before interest and taxes.
6. Financial Income and Expenses—interest, gains/losses from financial operations.
7. Profit Before Taxes (EBT).
8. Income Tax—expected tax obligation.
9. Net Income—the resulting profit after taxes.

The budgeted income statement does not exist in isolation. It is closely linked to sales planning (revenue forecasts), cost calculations (e.g., using full or variable costing), cost center budgets, cash flow budgeting (expected inflows and outflows), and budgeted balance sheet (to evaluate profitability and asset structure).

The budgeted income statement allows companies to:

- Plan their financial results,
- Monitor variances between actual and planned results (variance analysis),
- Allocate responsibility across departments (e.g., via cost center income statements),
- Simulate different scenarios (optimistic, realistic, pessimistic),
- Evaluate business performance and cost efficiency.

Forms of the Budgeted Income Statement

There are two main forms of the budgeted income statement:

1. By cost center—focuses on the performance of individual organizational units.
2. By product/performance—analyzes the profitability of individual products or services.

Both forms offer valuable insights for decision-making at various levels of management.

The budgeted income statement is a fundamental controlling tool used to manage a company's profitability. It provides a forward-looking view and enables businesses not only to monitor but also to proactively influence financial outcomes. Its purpose is not just to estimate future profit but to identify how that profit can be realistically achieved.

From Practice: Budgeted Income Statement in an Electronics Manufacturing Company

Company Context:

An electronics manufacturing company, *ElectroTech Industries*, plans to launch a new line of smart thermostats in the upcoming financial year. In preparation, the company creates a budgeted income statement to support financial planning, investor communication, and operational decision-making.

Objective:

To project the profitability of the new product line and ensure alignment with the company's overall financial goals.

Budget Assumptions:
- Sales volume: 50,000 units
- Selling price per unit: €120
- Variable cost per unit: €70
- Fixed operating expenses: €1,200,000
- Tax rate: 19%

Budgeted Income Statement:

Item	Amount (€)
Sales revenue	6,000,000
Variable costs	3,500,000
Contribution margin	2,500,000
Fixed operating expenses	1,200,000
Operating profit (EBIT)	1,300,000
Income tax (19%)	247,000
Net profit	1,053,000

Insights & Impact:

- The budgeted net profit of over €1 million confirms the financial viability of the product.
- Managers used this report to justify investments in new production equipment.
- Marketing and logistics teams were given specific sales and distribution targets.
- The budgeted figures provided a basis for monthly variance analysis during the year to track actual performance.

Accurate forecasting of both variable and fixed costs is crucial for strategic pricing. Regular updates to the budget helped the company remain agile in response to supply chain disruptions. The use of a contribution margin approach clarified the impact of cost changes on profitability.

Budgeted Cash Flow Statement

The budgeted cash flow statement is a key tool in financial planning and liquidity management. Unlike the income statement, which works with revenues and expenses, the cash flow budget captures the actual movement of cash over time, i.e., cash inflows and outflows. Its primary purpose is to ensure that the company has sufficient cash available at all times to meet its obligations while also utilizing any surplus funds effectively.

The cash flow budget provides an overview of the sources of cash inflows and how cash is spent. This allows companies to anticipate timing mismatches between receipts and payments, plan their financing, assess investment projects, and identify risks related to liquidity shortages.

The budgeted cash flow is typically divided into three main categories, in line with the structure of the cash flow statement used in international financial reporting standards (IFRS):

1. Operating Activities
   This section covers the core business activities, such as cash receipts from sales of goods or services, payments to suppliers, employee wages, and taxes. The key question here is whether the business can generate sufficient cash from its operations to cover its expenses without relying on external financing.
2. Investing Activities
   This part includes cash flows related to the acquisition or sale of long-term assets—such as purchasing machinery, selling properties, or expenses for development. These flows are often negative, as they represent investments in the company's future.
3. Financing Activities
   This section reflects cash inflows from loans, issuing shares, or other financing sources, and outflows for loan repayments, interest payments, or dividend distributions. It serves to manage the company's capital structure and ensure liquidity when cash from operations or investments is insufficient.

The budgeted cash flow can be prepared using:

- The direct method, which is based directly on the forecasted receipts and payments in each category; or
- The indirect method, which starts from the forecasted net income and adjusts it for non-cash items and changes in working capital.

Benefits of the Cash Flow Budget are early identification of potential liquidity issues, ability to optimize corporate financing, strengthened coordination between departments (e.g., purchasing, sales, and finance), support for strategic decision-making (e.g., investments, expansions, credit policy).

A well-prepared cash flow budget becomes a critical controlling tool, ensuring the company's financial stability, health, and flexibility in a rapidly changing environment.

From Practice: Budgeted Cash Flow in a Manufacturing Company
Company Context:

A medium-sized company specializing in the production of eco-friendly packaging products, with seasonal fluctuations in demand (higher in Q2 and Q3). The business relies on timely delivery of raw materials and swift fulfillment of customer orders.

Challenge:

At the beginning of the year, the financial controller noticed a mismatch between planned production increases and available liquidity. While the profit and loss budget showed healthy profitability, the cash flow budget revealed a liquidity shortfall expected in Q2, due to high upfront material costs and slow payment cycles from customers.

Solution—Use of Budgeted Cash Flow:

1. Detailed Cash Flow Forecast:

   The controller prepared a monthly cash flow budget, breaking down cash inflows and outflows across operating, investing, and financing activities.
2. Key Findings:
   - A significant cash outflow in April due to advance payments for biodegradable materials.
   - Customer payments delayed until mid-June due to 60-day payment terms.
   - A planned equipment upgrade in May would further reduce available cash.
3. Decisions Based on the Cash Flow Budget:
   - The investment in new equipment was postponed to September, when cash inflows were expected to peak.
   - The company negotiated partial deliveries and payments with suppliers, smoothing out the April outflow.
   - A short-term credit line was arranged with the bank for Q2, to bridge the temporary liquidity gap.
   - Customer incentives were introduced to encourage early payments (e.g., 2% discount for payments within 30 days).
4. Result:
   - The company avoided a liquidity crisis.
   - It maintained its production schedule without delays.
   - The actual cash position stayed within 95% of the budgeted forecasts.
   - The cash flow budget became a regularly used tool in monthly management meetings.

While profitability is crucial, cash availability is vital for ensuring smooth operations. The budgeted cash flow helped management identify timing risks early, take proactive steps, and maintain financial flexibility, despite seasonal challenges.

2.11 Strategic Maps and KPI Linkage

In the modern performance management environment, it is not enough to simply measure financial outcomes. Organizations must understand *how* and *why* these results occur, and what strategic drivers contribute to long-term success. Strategic maps (also known as strategy maps) have emerged as a powerful visual and conceptual tool to support this objective.

Strategy maps help organizations articulate their strategy in a structured way by showing the cause-and-effect relationships between strategic objectives across different perspectives. They originate from the Balanced Scorecard framework, but their use has expanded well beyond it, becoming a central element of strategic controlling.

A strategic map typically aligns with four key perspectives: financial, customer, internal processes, and learning & growth. Each objective within these perspectives is linked to one or more Key Performance Indicators (KPIs), which are used to measure progress and performance. These KPIs are not selected in isolation. They are chosen for their ability to explain, support, or predict the achievement of higher-level strategic goals.

By laying out these relationships visually, strategy maps clarify how intangible drivers, such as employee engagement, innovation, or customer satisfaction, lead to tangible outcomes like revenue growth, cost reduction, or return on capital employed. This fosters alignment throughout the organization, as all employees can see how their actions contribute to broader objectives.

For example, a company may have a financial goal to increase profitability. To achieve this, it might set a customer objective to improve satisfaction. The customer satisfaction goal might depend on improving service delivery, which is an internal process objective. Achieving better service delivery might, in turn, require improved training and knowledge sharing, which falls under the learning and growth perspective. KPIs such as "Average Training Hours per Employee," "Service Error Rate," and "Net Promoter Score" could then be used to measure progress across each level.

Strategic maps are especially useful in bridging the gap between strategy formulation and execution. They allow decision-makers to:

- Communicate strategy clearly across the organization
- Align departmental goals with enterprise-wide strategy
- Identify performance gaps early through KPI monitoring
- Adjust initiatives and resources in response to performance feedback

Moreover, the process of designing a strategy map encourages leadership teams to make their assumptions explicit. It stimulates discussion about what truly drives success in their specific context and helps reveal missing links, unrealistic expectations, or competing objectives.

In controlling, the value of strategic maps lies in their ability to provide structure to non-financial performance measurement. While traditional financial statements report *what happened*, strategic maps help answer *why it happened* and *what to do next*. They turn the controller's role from a reporter of outcomes into a facilitator of strategic execution.

KPI linkage, when done properly, ensures that metrics across different business units are not isolated but support one another. This prevents siloed behavior and encourages collaboration toward shared results. Furthermore, integrating strategic maps into performance reviews, budgeting processes, and bonus schemes helps to reinforce strategic alignment throughout the year.

In today's rapidly changing business environment, having a clearly defined strategic map supported by well-designed KPIs is no longer optional. It is an essential part of an agile and responsive performance management system that allows companies to stay focused on their strategic direction while adapting quickly to new challenges.

From Practice: Implementing Strategic Maps and KPI Linkage in a Manufacturing Company

A mid-sized industrial equipment manufacturer based in Central Europe was facing stagnating growth despite stable financial results. Management recognized that financial metrics alone were not providing enough insight into the root causes of this stagnation. They decided to implement a more structured performance management system centered around strategic maps and aligned KPIs.

The company began by organizing strategic workshops with the executive team and key functional leaders. Together, they defined the company's long-term vision: to become the most responsive and quality-driven supplier in their market segment. Based on this vision, they developed a strategic map organized into four perspectives: Financial, Customer, Internal Processes, and Learning & Growth.

Within the financial perspective, one of the primary objectives was to increase the return on invested capital. In the customer perspective, the key objective was to improve customer satisfaction and delivery reliability. For internal processes, the focus was on reducing production lead time and improving quality control. Finally, in the learning & growth perspective, the company identified employee training and digital system upgrades as essential enablers.

Each of these strategic objectives was assigned measurable KPIs. For example:

- Return on Invested Capital (ROIC) and Operating Margin under the Financial perspective
- On-Time Delivery Rate and Customer Complaint Rate for the Customer perspective
- First Pass Yield and Average Lead Time for Internal Processes
- Training Hours per Employee and ERP System Utilization Rate for Learning & Growth

The company integrated the strategic map and KPIs into its monthly reporting structure and annual budgeting cycle. Managers were trained to interpret and act on these indicators, and strategic review meetings were introduced quarterly to monitor progress.

After 18 months, the company observed significant improvements. Customer satisfaction scores increased by 15%, production lead times were reduced by 20%, and the return on invested capital rose by 2.5 percentage points. Moreover, employee engagement improved, as teams better understood how their work contributed to broader company goals.

One key success factor was the visual and communicative power of the strategy map. It helped align all departments and reinforced the link between day-to-day activities and strategic outcomes. The leadership team reported that decision-making had become more proactive, data-driven, and focused on long-term value creation.

This demonstrates how strategic maps, when supported by well-chosen KPIs, can transform performance management into a more integrated and future-oriented process.

It also highlights the evolving role of controllers—from financial record-keepers to strategic partners.

2.12 Controlling in the Digital Age

In the era of digital transformation, all business functions are undergoing significant changes, and controlling is no exception. Traditional approaches to planning, budgeting, analysis, and reporting are being enhanced or replaced by modern digital solutions that enable faster, more accurate, and more strategic decision-making. Controlling is evolving from a reactive support function into a proactive business partner that not only analyzes the past but also helps shape the future.

Historically, the role of the controller was primarily focused on cost control and reporting. Today, however, the controller is increasingly seen as a strategic partner to management. This new role involves interpreting complex data, forecasting future developments, evaluating potential business scenarios, and providing valuable insights that guide strategic decisions. Modern controllers work across departments and are closely involved in operations, marketing, and human resources, ensuring that financial perspectives are embedded in all areas of the business.

Foundations of Digital Controlling

The foundation of digital controlling lies in integrated systems and tools that allow real-time access to data and seamless information flow across departments. Enterprise Resource Planning (ERP) systems such as SAP, Oracle, or Microsoft Dynamics serve as the backbone, consolidating financial and operational data into one platform. These systems support effective budgeting, forecasting, and performance analysis by providing timely and reliable data.

Business Intelligence (BI) tools like Power BI, Tableau, and QlikView play a crucial role in enabling visualization and analysis. They allow controllers to create dynamic dashboards that monitor key performance indicators, identify trends in revenues and costs, and analyze variances. This helps management respond quickly to changes and make informed decisions.

Another important development is the automation of routine processes through Robotic Process Automation (RPA). Controllers can automate data collection, invoice validation, and internal checks, thereby reducing manual errors and freeing up time for strategic analysis. In addition, cloud-based platforms such as Jedox, Anaplan, or Workday Adaptive Planning allow collaborative, real-time financial planning accessible from anywhere.

With the advancement of artificial intelligence and machine learning, controllers are also adopting predictive and prescriptive analytics. These techniques make it possible to forecast future outcomes based on historical data and to recommend optimal decisions under different scenarios. For example, predictive models can anticipate changes in cash flow, sales volumes, or raw material costs, while prescriptive tools suggest actions to optimize pricing or cost structures.

Benefits and Limits of Digital Controlling

One of the key benefits of digital controlling is the acceleration of planning cycles. Forecasts that once took weeks to prepare can now be updated in real time. This leads to greater agility and responsiveness to market dynamics. Moreover, automation reduces operational costs and improves the accuracy of results. By involving more departments in the planning process and leveraging interactive reporting tools, companies can foster a more transparent and collaborative business environment.

Another major advantage is the increased use of data-driven decision-making. With more accurate and up-to-date information, managers can evaluate risks and opportunities with greater confidence. Digital controlling also supports long-term strategic initiatives, such as sustainability reporting or ESG compliance, by providing reliable and auditable data.

Despite its advantages, digital controlling also presents several challenges. Implementing advanced technologies can be costly and time-consuming. It requires not only investment in software but also organizational change, new skills, and revised processes. Controllers must embrace continuous learning to keep up with data analytics, information systems, and evolving business models.

Another challenge lies in data quality. Even the most sophisticated tools are ineffective if the underlying data is incomplete, inconsistent, or inaccurate. Therefore, establishing robust data governance and ensuring cross-departmental cooperation is critical.

Moreover, the transformation of the controller's role means moving beyond numbers. Communication skills, business acumen, and the ability to translate complex data into clear narratives become essential.

In the digital age, controllers are no longer just financial analysts. They become stewards of corporate data, bridging the gap between technology and business strategy. They help shape a data-driven culture by promoting the use of analytics in everyday decision-making. Their goal is not only to report what happened, but to explain why it happened, what might happen next, and what should be done.

2.13 Behavioral Controlling and the Psychology of Decision-Making

In addition to technical and analytical competencies, controlling also involves understanding the human side of decision-making. Behavioral controlling focuses on how psychological, emotional, and social factors influence the planning, budgeting, and evaluation processes within organizations. It recognizes that decision-makers are not always entirely rational and that their choices are often shaped by biases, perception errors, and group dynamics.

While traditional controlling models assume that managers and employees act logically and in pursuit of optimal financial outcomes, real-world decisions are often influenced by factors such as stress, intuition, incomplete information, or corporate culture. Behavioral controlling thus serves as a complementary discipline that enriches financial data with psychological insights, helping to improve the quality of decisions and communication across the organization.

The Role of Psychology in Controlling

Human behavior plays a crucial role in the success or failure of controlling systems. Even the most accurate calculations or well-designed performance indicators can lead to poor results if people interpret them incorrectly or react emotionally. Understanding the psychological background of how decisions are made allows controllers to anticipate potential resistance, improve forecasting reliability, and design more effective incentive systems.

Controllers are frequently involved in budget negotiations, performance evaluations, and investment decisions. These situations are often emotionally charged and subject to subjective judgments. A manager under pressure may underestimate future risks or overstate expected returns. An employee might manipulate data to achieve a bonus target. Behavioral controlling helps identify and mitigate these risks.

Key psychological aspects relevant to controlling include:

- Cognitive biases, such as confirmation bias, anchoring, or overconfidence, which distort how information is interpreted.
- Motivation and incentives, which influence performance and behavior. Poorly designed reward systems can encourage short-term thinking or even unethical conduct.
- Group dynamics and communication, particularly in team settings where conformity or groupthink may suppress critical thinking.
- Perception of fairness, especially in cost allocation, performance appraisal, and resource distribution.

Understanding these factors enables controllers to design processes that are not only financially sound but also psychologically robust.

Behavioral Aspects in Planning and Budgeting

Budgeting is not only a technical process but also a behavioral one. People involved in budgeting tend to behave strategically. They may deliberately understate expected revenues or overstate costs in order to secure more favorable budgets. This phenomenon is known as "budgetary slack."

Similarly, rolling forecasts can be biased if employees consistently provide conservative estimates to ensure that targets are easily achieved. Behavioral controlling addresses these tendencies by promoting transparency, encouraging honest communication, and aligning planning with individual and team motivations.

One approach is to separate target setting from resource planning to prevent conflicts of interest. Another is to involve employees in the budgeting process more actively, increasing their ownership and accountability.

Performance Measurement and Behavioral Impact

The way performance is measured and presented greatly affects how people respond. If key performance indicators (KPIs) are perceived as unrealistic, employees may feel discouraged or even ignore them. On the other hand, well-chosen KPIs can motivate, align actions with strategy, and foster a sense of achievement.

Controllers must therefore balance financial targets with behavioral consequences. This includes considering whether incentives are too narrowly focused, whether they might encourage manipulation, or whether non-financial indicators (such as customer satisfaction or employee engagement) might provide a fuller picture.

Moreover, performance evaluations should not only focus on results but also on behavior and effort. This helps prevent a purely output-oriented culture and fosters ethical and long-term decision-making.

The Controller as a Facilitator of Dialogue

In many companies, controllers act as intermediaries between management and operational departments. Their role requires a high level of emotional intelligence, as they often deliver difficult messages—such as cost cuts or performance shortfalls—and must do so in a way that maintains trust and cooperation.

Behavioral controlling equips controllers with the tools to better manage these conversations. Active listening, empathy, and the ability to frame data in a way that resonates with different audiences are all key competencies. This human-centered approach enhances the controller's role as a strategic partner rather than a "policeman."

2.14 ESG and Sustainability in Controlling

In recent years, environmental, social, and governance (ESG) factors have become integral to how businesses measure performance and long-term success. Controlling, traditionally focused on financial performance and efficiency, is now evolving to support a broader and more sustainable value creation framework. This shift reflects not only societal expectations but also investor requirements, regulatory changes, and competitive dynamics.

Modern controlling must account for non-financial indicators that reflect a company's environmental impact, social responsibility, and ethical governance. Integrating ESG into controlling expands its role from a cost-centered perspective to one that enables sustainable decision-making and long-term strategic resilience.

The Expanding Role of Controlling in ESG

Traditionally, controllers focused on budgeting, cost analysis, and financial reporting. However, the inclusion of ESG criteria means that controlling must now support sustainability strategies, ensure data transparency, and contribute to integrated reporting frameworks. This evolution requires the development of new metrics, systems, and competencies.

Controllers are now involved in measuring e.g. carbon emissions and environmental impact, diversity and inclusion efforts, health and safety performance, ethical sourcing and supply chain transparency, or board diversity and corporate governance.

These indicators are not just supplementary. They increasingly influence capital allocation, risk assessments, and even brand reputation. Controlling must therefore become a bridge between financial logic and sustainable value creation.

ESG Metrics in the Controlling System

The integration of ESG into the controlling system begins with the identification of relevant key performance indicators (KPIs). These KPIs must reflect the company's strategic sustainability goals and be measurable, verifiable, and comparable over time.

Some common ESG indicators include:

- Environmental: energy consumption, CO_2 footprint, water usage, recycling rate
- Social: employee turnover, gender pay gap, community investments
- Governance: compliance incidents, whistleblower reports, board structure

Incorporating these metrics into dashboards, scorecards, and performance evaluations allows for their regular monitoring and integration into planning and decision-making processes.

Integrated Reporting and Communication

ESG reporting must be transparent, reliable, and aligned with recognized frameworks such as the Global Reporting Initiative (GRI), Sustainability Accounting Standards Board (SASB), or the EU Corporate Sustainability Reporting Directive (CSRD). Controllers play a key role in gathering, verifying, and presenting ESG data in a consistent and decision-relevant format.

Integrated reports, which combine financial and non-financial data, are increasingly expected by investors and regulators. The controller's responsibility is to ensure data consistency, avoid greenwashing, and present ESG outcomes in the broader context of business performance.

Risk Management and ESG

ESG factors are also closely tied to corporate risk management. Environmental risks (such as climate change or resource scarcity), social risks (like labor unrest or reputation damage), and governance risks (such as regulatory non-compliance) can all have significant financial consequences. Controllers must assess these risks and incorporate them into scenario planning, stress testing, and strategic analysis.

By identifying and quantifying ESG risks, controlling can help develop mitigation strategies, such as diversifying suppliers, investing in low-carbon technologies, or enhancing transparency.

2.15 Risk Controlling

Risk controlling has become an essential part of modern management systems, particularly in environments characterized by volatility, complexity, and rapid change. In contrast to traditional risk management, which often focused only on financial or operational risks in isolation, modern risk controlling is about integrating risk assessment and control mechanisms directly into planning, budgeting, and performance monitoring processes.

Quantification of Risks and Their Impact on Budgets

One of the primary responsibilities of risk controlling is to quantify potential risks and evaluate their impact on financial plans, especially on budgets. This involves not only identifying potential risk factors, such as price volatility, supply chain disruptions, or changes in customer demand, but also assessing the likelihood and potential magnitude of these risks.

Once risks have been identified and quantified, their potential effects must be incorporated into the company's budgeting framework. Instead of working with single-point estimates, risk-adjusted budgets use ranges or probabilistic forecasts. For example, instead of budgeting for a fixed sales volume or cost, the company might define a base case, optimistic case, and pessimistic case. This approach allows management to understand budgetary sensitivity and prepare for contingencies.

Risk controlling also supports the development of risk buffers within budgets. These might take the form of contingency reserves, flexible cost structures, or dynamic investment prioritization that can be adjusted as new information becomes available.

The Relationship Between Controlling and Enterprise Risk Management (ERM)

Risk controlling is closely linked to the broader framework of Enterprise Risk Management (ERM). While ERM focuses on the identification, assessment, and strategic management of risks across the entire organization, risk controlling adds a quantitative and financial dimension to this process. Controllers play a critical role in translating risk assessments into financial terms, which can then be integrated into strategic planning, operational decision-making, and reporting.

In a well-integrated system, risk controlling provides the financial logic to ERM's strategic perspective. It ensures that risk considerations are embedded not only in the company's strategic goals but also in its operational plans and key performance indicators. This integration enables companies to move from a reactive risk posture to a proactive and informed risk-taking culture that supports long-term value creation.

Furthermore, risk controlling contributes to the monitoring of risk-bearing capacity, i.e., the ability of the company to absorb losses without jeopardizing its solvency or strategic objectives. This includes stress-testing financial assumptions and evaluating the interdependence of multiple risks on overall business performance.

Simulation Techniques in Risk Controlling

A particularly powerful set of tools in risk controlling involves simulation techniques, which help model complex, uncertain environments. Two of the most frequently used methods are Monte Carlo simulation and scenario analysis.

Monte Carlo simulation uses statistical sampling techniques to model the probability distribution of outcomes. By running thousands of simulations with random inputs (within defined probability distributions), the company can generate a full risk profile for key financial outcomes such as EBIT, cash flow, or ROI. This method is particularly useful for quantifying uncertainty in areas like project investments, foreign exchange exposure, or commodity pricing.

Scenario analysis, by contrast, is based on the definition of coherent, internally consistent narratives of future developments. Unlike the Monte Carlo approach, which relies on large numbers of random inputs, scenario analysis typically explores a limited number of well-designed cases: for instance, a best case, worst case, and most likely case. These scenarios allow management to evaluate the potential impact of external shocks (e.g., economic downturns, regulatory changes, supply chain crises) on the company's strategic and operational plans.

Both techniques can be used in combination. While scenario analysis helps identify the major uncertainties and drivers of change, Monte Carlo simulations can then provide a quantitative analysis of the likelihood and potential financial impact of these uncertainties.

Risk controlling ensures that insights gained from these simulations are not merely academic but are translated into concrete decisions—such as adjusting investment strategies, hedging operations, or creating dynamic budgeting structures. Moreover, simulation outputs can be directly linked to performance dashboards and early warning indicators, enabling real-time monitoring of emerging risks.

From Practice: Integrating Risk Controlling into Budgeting through Monte Carlo Simulation

A European manufacturing company specializing in industrial automation decided to integrate risk controlling into its annual budgeting process. Historically, the company had prepared single-scenario budgets based on average forecasts of sales volumes, raw material prices, and labor costs. However, frequent deviations between planned and actual results led to significant budget variances, undermining managerial trust in the planning process.

To improve reliability, the controlling department, in cooperation with the enterprise risk management team, introduced a Monte Carlo simulation model as part of the financial planning cycle.

The process began with identifying key risk variables that significantly affected the company's profitability: customer demand, steel prices, exchange rates (EUR/USD), and production downtimes. For each variable, historical data was used to define probability distributions, normal for demand volatility, triangular for commodity prices, and discrete for exchange rates based on macroeconomic scenarios.

The controller created a simulation model for EBITDA that incorporated these variables. The Monte Carlo ran 10,000 iterations, generating a probability distribution of expected EBITDA values. The simulation output showed that while the base case projected an EBITDA of €15 million, there was a 20% probability that EBITDA could fall below €10 million, mainly due to raw material cost spikes and demand downturns.

Based on these results, management took several actions:

- A contingency buffer of €1 million was added to the operating expense budget.
- A new hedging strategy for steel procurement was implemented to limit exposure to price volatility.
- Customer contracts were adjusted to include price-adjustment clauses triggered by input cost changes.
- An early warning dashboard was established, tracking real-time movements in the key risk variables used in the simulation.

In the following year, despite raw material prices rising sharply in Q2, the company remained within budgeted profit margins, largely due to proactive hedging and pricing adjustments. The CFO reported improved confidence in the planning process, and the Board requested that Monte Carlo simulations be extended to investment planning and liquidity forecasting.

2.16 Controlling in Different Types of Organizations

Controlling, as a managerial function, plays a vital role across various types of organizations, but its specific application and focus differ significantly depending on the sector and core activities of the entity. Understanding these distinctions is essential for aligning controlling tools with strategic objectives and operational realities.

Controlling in Manufacturing vs. Trading Companies

In manufacturing companies, controlling is heavily oriented toward cost management, production efficiency, and capacity utilization. A central focus lies in the planning, monitoring, and analysis of production costs—both direct and indirect. The structure of cost accounting is typically more complex, involving detailed cost center hierarchies, activity-based costing, and standard costing systems. Performance measurement in manufacturing emphasizes unit costs, contribution margins, overall equipment effectiveness (OEE), and productivity indicators.

Conversely, in trading companies, the core of controlling shifts toward inventory turnover, gross margin analysis, and working capital management. Since there is no production, the emphasis is placed on optimizing procurement, logistics, and sales operations. Controlling supports decision-making related to pricing strategies, product mix optimization, and supplier performance. The key performance indicators (KPIs) here often include stock turnover ratios, order fulfillment rates, and profitability by product or customer segment.

Controlling in Service Organizations

In service-oriented organizations, the main challenge of controlling lies in the intangibility of the outputs. Unlike manufacturing or trading, services are not stored, and quality is often perceived subjectively. As such, controlling in this sector focuses on time utilization, staff productivity, service quality, and customer satisfaction. Personnel costs tend to represent the largest portion of expenses, making labor efficiency and allocation a key area of cost control.

Controlling tools must be adapted to capture both quantitative and qualitative aspects of performance. For example, in consulting firms, KPIs might include billable hours, utilization rates, and client retention, while in healthcare, controlling may monitor costs per patient, treatment effectiveness, and resource usage.

Controlling in Non-profit Organizations and Public Administration

Non-profit organizations and public sector entities present a unique context for controlling, as their objectives are not driven by profit but by social value creation or public service delivery. In these organizations, financial controlling focuses on budget adherence, cost-effectiveness, and accountability rather than profitability. Performance measurement frameworks often include output-based budgeting, impact assessments, and efficiency ratios.

A growing number of public institutions are adopting modern controlling tools, such as performance-based budgeting, balanced scorecards, and benchmarking, to increase transparency and improve service quality. However, the implementation is often challenged by bureaucratic constraints, limited flexibility in financial planning, and a complex network of stakeholders.

In the case of non-profits, controlling also supports donor reporting, grant compliance, and impact evaluation, often requiring a dual focus on both financial and mission-driven performance indicators.

Cost Management and Performance Measurement Specifics

The nature of cost structures and performance metrics varies widely across organizations. Manufacturing firms typically have high fixed costs and require precise overhead allocation, while trading companies must manage low-margin, high-volume business models. Service organizations, by contrast, deal with highly variable human resource costs and face challenges in measuring output per unit of input.

Performance measurement must also reflect the strategic focus of the organization. While private enterprises prioritize profitability, return on investment, and growth, public sector institutions may emphasize efficiency, citizen satisfaction, and policy impact. This necessitates a customized set of KPIs and a flexible approach to controlling design.

Chapter 3
Objectives and Methodology

The first major part of this monograph is devoted to building a comprehensive theoretical framework that serves as the foundation for understanding controlling as a modern managerial tool for steering business processes. In this section, controlling is not only defined as a system for measurement and monitoring, but also as a coordinating and information-based concept that supports effective decision-making across all management levels.

Emphasis is placed on the integration of controlling with other key business areas, particularly financial management, strategic planning, and operational control. The evolution of controlling is traced from its origins in Anglo-American practice to its present-day form within the European context, including its specific development within the Czech business environment. Special attention is given to the role of the controller as a strategic partner to management, who not only provides data but also interprets it and proposes actionable solutions.

The chapter also clarifies the often-confused distinction between controlling and management accounting, aiming to establish a clearer understanding of the purpose and methodology of each discipline.

A substantial portion of the theoretical discussion is dedicated to the classification and analysis of controlling tools, which are systematically divided into strategic and operational instruments. This section lays the methodological foundation for the subsequent empirical research and enables a direct comparison between theoretical concepts and their practical application in organizations.

The second major part of the monograph presents the empirical findings, which are based on a comprehensive survey of companies in the Czech Republic. The research aimed to assess the implementation levels of various controlling tools across different industries, company sizes, and ownership structures. The collected primary data was subsequently enriched by financial indicators extracted from the Albertina Gold Edition database, thereby enhancing the analytical depth of the study.

This integration allowed for a more robust evaluation of the relationship between the use of controlling tools and company performance, not only through absolute

M. Vlčková, *Controlling as a Business Process Management Tool*, Contributions to Finance and Accounting, https://doi.org/10.1007/978-3-032-27526-4_3

figures such as assets, revenue, and profit, but also via classic financial ratios such as profitability (ROA, ROE), liquidity, indebtedness, and operating cash flow. This methodological approach significantly improves the validity and practical relevance of the research outcomes.

3.1 Objectives of the Monograph

The main objective of this monograph is to define controlling as a systemic and coordinating concept that integrates planning, monitoring, reporting, and decision-making within the organization. Particular attention is devoted to the analysis of specific controlling tools, both strategic and operational, and their impact on business performance and efficiency.

The partial goals include:

- Evaluating the current level of controlling implementation in Czech enterprises within the context of the contemporary economic and technological landscape.
- Analyzing the relationship between controlling and key financial indicators, including identifying common weaknesses and risks in controlling practices.
- Proposing measures for optimizing the controlling process, with a focus on data integration, decision support, and predictive analytics.
- Formulating recommendations for companies that aim to implement or further develop controlling, tailored to their size, sector, and available resources.

The output of the monograph is a comprehensive perspective on controlling as a dynamic and adaptable tool that can significantly enhance the competitiveness of Czech enterprises. Additionally, the study lays the groundwork for future research, particularly in areas such as digital transformation of controlling, automation of reporting processes, and the integration of advanced data analytics.

3.2 Methodology

Fulfillment of the above-mentioned objective will be achieved through the application of scientific methods such as observation, inquiry, analysis, synthesis, logical induction, deduction, description, and comparison. As part of the statistical analysis, a non-parametric statistical test will be employed.

Based on the questionnaire survey, controlling activities within enterprises will first be analyzed, and a discussion will be held regarding which controlling methods (both operational and strategic) are most frequently utilized in practice. The data obtained from the survey will subsequently be linked with financial data retrieved from the Albertina Gold Edition database. The examined enterprises will then be analyzed in relation to financial indicators derived from their balance sheets and profit and loss statements.

On the basis of the above-mentioned analyses and statistical testing, recommendations will be formulated for different types of enterprises (categorized by number of employees and annual turnover).

In the first step, it is necessary to determine whether the analyzed enterprises have implemented strategic and operational controlling tools. These data were gathered through a questionnaire survey, in which a proportional sample of over 12,900 enterprises was constructed to reflect the distribution of companies in the Czech Republic. In total, responses were obtained from 245 enterprises, resulting in a response rate of nearly 2%.

In the next step, financial data for these classified companies were collected and evaluated. Unfortunately, it was not possible to obtain financial data from all 245 enterprises; complete financial information was available only for 160 enterprises.

Subsequently, the relationships among these variables will be analyzed using statistical tests. First, a test for the normality of data distribution will be conducted using the Shapiro–Wilk test. This will be followed by testing for differences between groups based on the Mann–Whitney U test.

1. *Testing for Normality of Data Distribution*

To identify differences in financial performance between companies engaged in traditional retail ("retail") and those operating in the e-commerce sector ("e-commerce"), a comparative quantitative analysis was conducted based on a set of key financial indicators. Before testing the hypotheses, it was necessary to verify whether the analyzed data followed a normal distribution, which is a prerequisite for the application of most parametric tests. Normality is a key assumption for many parametric statistical tests (such as the t-test), which rely on the premise that the data are drawn from a normally distributed population (Field, 2018).

To test for normality, the Shapiro–Wilk test was employed (Shapiro & Wilk, 1965). This test is widely recognized as one of the most sensitive and accurate tests for assessing normality in practical applications. It evaluates whether a sample distribution deviates significantly from a theoretical normal distribution by analyzing discrepancies between observed and expected values. If the p-value is less than 0.05, the null hypothesis of normality is rejected (the data are not normally distributed). If the p-value is equal to or greater than 0.05, we fail to reject the null hypothesis (the data may be normally distributed).

2. *Testing Differences Between Groups*

To analyze differences in financial indicators between two independent groups of firms ("retail" and "e-commerce"), the Mann–Whitney U test will be used. This test is a non-parametric alternative to the independent-samples t-test, which does not require the assumption of normally distributed data or equal variances between groups (Nachar, 2008). It evaluates whether the distributions of a given variable differ significantly between two independent samples and is particularly appropriate when the assumption of normality is violated, as confirmed by the Shapiro–Wilk test.

The variables may not correspond to Gaussian normal distribution at the same time; it is sufficient to assume that they are continuous. The test involves the calculation of a statistic, usually called U, whose distribution under the null hypothesis is known. U is then given by (Devore, 2015):

$$U_1 = R_1 - \frac{n_1(n_1+1)}{2}, \tag{3.1}$$

where n_1 is the sample size for sample 1, and R_1 is the sum of the ranks in sample 1. An equally valid formula for U is:

$$U_2 = R_2 - \frac{n_2(n_2+1)}{2} \tag{3.2}$$

The smaller value of U1 and U2 is the one used when consulting significance tables. The sum of the two values is given by:

$$U_1 + U_2 = R_1 - \frac{n_1(n_1+1)}{2} + R_2 - \frac{n_2(n_2+1)}{2} \tag{3.3}$$

Knowing that $R_1 + R_2 = \frac{N(N+1)}{2}$ and $N = n_1 + n_2$, and doing some algebra, we find that the sum is $U_1 + U_2 = n_1 n_2$.

The statistical hypothesis for the test is defined as follows:

- H_0 (null hypothesis): the distribution of the variable is the same across both groups (equal medians),
- H_1 (alternative hypothesis): the distribution of the variable differs between groups (unequal medians).

The test will be applied individually to each financial indicator. Results will be interpreted at a significance level of $\alpha = 0.05$. Variables with *p*-values less than 0.05 will be considered to differ significantly between the groups.

Chapter 4
Empirical Findings

Controlling has become an indispensable part of the management process, particularly in medium-sized and large enterprises. Over recent years, however, the implementation of controlling systems, or at least the adoption of basic controlling elements and tools, has also become increasingly evident in small businesses, and even micro-enterprises. This trend suggests a growing awareness of the importance of financial and operational oversight across the entire business spectrum, regardless of company size.

In the first stage of the empirical analysis, data from 245 enterprises were evaluated. These enterprises were classified according to whether or not they had implemented controlling as a management tool. The classification was carried out based on three key dimensions: the number of employees, the region (NUTS3 level) in which the business is located, and the type of enterprise (i.e. manufacturing, trade, or services).

The following figure presents a comparison of the number of employees in companies that have implemented controlling and those that have not. The visualized data clearly indicate that in all size categories based on the number of employees, enterprises with established controlling systems outnumber those without them. This supports the hypothesis that controlling is more prevalent among larger firms, where complexity and volume of activities necessitate more robust management and control mechanisms.

The most significant differences can be observed in the 0–9 employees category and again in companies with over 100 employees. In the smallest category (0–9 employees), the difference implies that even micro-enterprises are beginning to adopt basic controlling methods, though the adoption rate remains relatively lower compared to larger categories.

A particularly striking finding appears in the 250–499 employee category, where 100% of the surveyed companies have implemented controlling. This indicates a complete saturation of controlling practices among upper medium-sized firms, where

M. Vlčková, *Controlling as a Business Process Management Tool*, Contributions to Finance and Accounting, https://doi.org/10.1007/978-3-032-27526-4_4

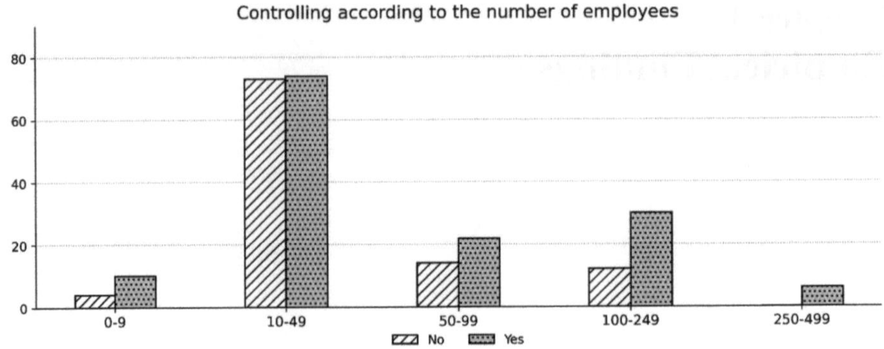

Fig. 4.1 Implementation of controlling by company size (number of employees). *Source* Own processing

the scale of operations almost mandates formalized control structures for effective decision-making, cost management, and performance measurement.[1]

The only group that yields ambiguous results is the 10–49 employee category. In this segment, the number of companies without controlling (73) is nearly equal to the number of companies with controlling (74). This statistical equilibrium suggests that this category may be a transition zone, where enterprises are either in the early stages of formalizing their internal processes or may be selectively adopting certain tools without fully embracing a comprehensive controlling system.

These results underscore the importance of company size as a determining factor in the implementation of controlling mechanisms. As the number of employees increases, so does the operational complexity, the number of internal processes, and the need for formalized management systems—factors which all significantly contribute to the adoption of controlling (Fig. 4.1).

The bar chart presented provides a comparative overview of the adoption of controlling practices across different types of businesses: commercial, services, manufacturing, and combined manufacturing and commercial operations. The data is categorized into two groups: businesses that have implemented controlling (represented in light green—"Yes") and those that have not (represented in blue—"No").

The manufacturing sector shows the highest adoption rate of controlling tools and methods among all business types. The green portion of the bar is significantly larger than the blue portion, indicating that the majority of manufacturing companies actively use controlling in their operations. This finding is consistent with expectations, as manufacturing businesses often deal with complex production processes, supply chains, and cost structures that necessitate rigorous planning, monitoring, and

[1] When preparing the questionnaire, it was assumed that companies with 500 employees or more have established controlling as a support tool for management. For this reason, the selection of companies was limited to the number of employees 0–499.

control mechanisms. These companies benefit greatly from controlling tools in areas such as cost management, capacity planning, and investment decision-making.

In the services sector, the adoption of controlling is also relatively strong, although less pronounced than in manufacturing. The bar is almost evenly split between those that use controlling and those that do not. This suggests a transitional stage in which many service-oriented firms recognize the value of controlling but may not have fully implemented it yet. Controlling in services can offer significant value, particularly in areas such as resource utilization, profitability analysis per client or project, and long-term financial planning. However, the less tangible nature of service outputs and generally lower capital intensity may explain the slower pace of adoption compared to manufacturing.

Commercial businesses (e.g., retail and wholesale) demonstrate the lowest overall use of controlling. While controlling is still present, the blue (No) portion represents a large share of the bar, implying a relatively limited adoption. This could be attributed to the traditionally transactional nature of commercial operations, where short-term sales and margin monitoring have been prioritized over strategic controlling approaches. Nonetheless, in an increasingly competitive retail environment, the lack of controlling tools may put these businesses at a disadvantage, especially in terms of optimizing inventory, supplier negotiations, and pricing strategies.

Interestingly, the combined manufacturing and commercial category shows a relatively balanced adoption of controlling, though the total number of companies in this category appears to be lower. This balance indicates a strategic blend: the manufacturing side of the business likely drives the need for controlling, while the commercial side may benefit from data-driven sales and distribution insights. These hybrid companies often require more integrated controlling systems to manage both production efficiency and market responsiveness.

Overall, the graph clearly illustrates that the more complex and production-oriented a business is, the more likely it is to implement controlling practices. Manufacturing businesses lead in adoption, followed by services and commercial enterprises. This trend underlines the importance of aligning controlling tools with the operational realities and strategic priorities of the business. As market dynamics evolve and data-driven decision-making becomes increasingly essential, it is expected that even sectors with traditionally low adoption rates, like commerce, will gradually increase their use of controlling methodologies (Fig. 4.2).

In the next step, the surveyed companies were classified according to their turnover into six categories, and an analysis was carried out to determine whether companies that have implemented controlling achieve higher levels of turnover compared to those that have not. This step is crucial because turnover reflects not only the company's market activity but also its ability to generate revenue and compete effectively within its industry.

For the purpose of this analysis, data from the quantitative research were used, focusing on 160 companies. However, it is important to note that not all respondents provided complete financial information. Out of the 160 companies, only 142 reported their total turnover, which forms the basis of the following evaluation.

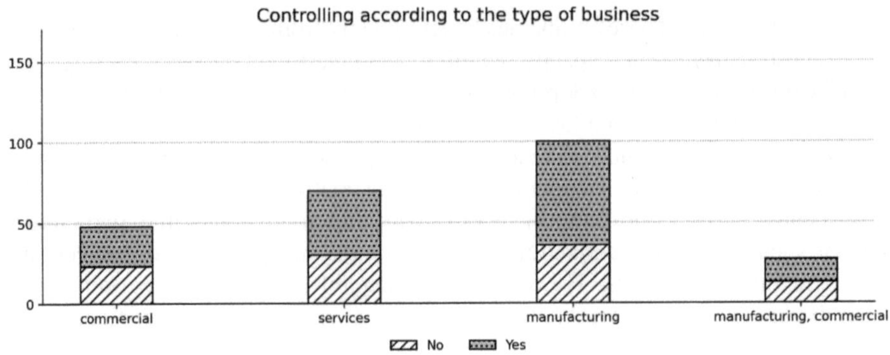

Fig. 4.2 Implementation of controlling in different types of businesses. *Source* Own processing

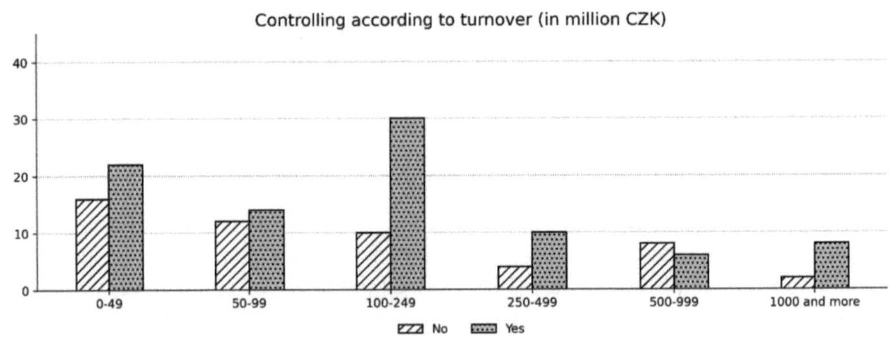

Fig. 4.3 Breakdown of companies by turnover. *Source* Own processing

The results are presented in both a chart and a table, allowing for a clear comparison across the six turnover categories. This enables us to observe whether there is a correlation between the existence of a controlling system and the company's financial performance in terms of sales revenue. Initial findings suggest that companies with controlling in place tend to fall more frequently into higher turnover categories, indicating that controlling may serve as an effective management tool for supporting financial growth (Fig. 4.3 and Table 4.1).

To ensure the robustness and appropriateness of the statistical testing applied in this analysis, the Shapiro–Wilk test was first conducted for the variable "total turnover" and for others financial variables for each group of companies; those with and without implemented controlling systems. The Shapiro–Wilk test is particularly suited for small to medium-sized datasets and is widely regarded for its sensitivity in detecting deviations from a normal distribution (Razali & Wah, 2011; Shapiro & Wilk, 1965). In this case, the results revealed that the distribution of turnover values in both groups significantly deviated from normality, with *p*-values below the significance threshold of 0.05. As a result, the null hypothesis of normal distribution was

Table 4.1 Controlling in relation to turnover category

Turnover category	Controlling implemented—No	Controlling implemented—Yes	Total
0–49 mil. CZK	16	22	38
50–99 mil. CZK	12	14	26
100–249 mil. CZK	10	30	40
250–499 mil. CZK	4	10	14
500–999 mil. CZK	8	6	14
1000 and more mil. CZK	2	8	10
Total	**52**	**90**	**142**

Source Own processing

rejected, and a non-parametric statistical method was required for further comparative analysis.

For a more detailed investigation of the relationship between company turnover and the implementation of controlling systems, the Mann–Whitney U test was subsequently employed. This non-parametric test is appropriate for comparing two independent groups (here, companies with controlling (Yes) and those without (No)) when the assumption of normality is not met. The test was conducted at a standard significance level of $\alpha = 0.05$.

The null hypothesis (H_0) stated that the medians of the two samples are equal ($\mu_1 - \mu_2 = 0$), while the alternative hypothesis (H_a) proposed that the medians differ ($\mu_1 - \mu_2 \neq 0$). The resulting *p*-value was 0.2202, which exceeds the defined significance level. Therefore, the null hypothesis could not be rejected, indicating that there is no statistically significant difference in turnover between companies that have implemented controlling and those that have not.

Based on this result, we cannot conclude that the presence of a controlling system has a measurable impact, either positive or negative,on the overall turnover of the companies in the sample. This finding underscores the complexity of business performance, suggesting that turnover is influenced by a broader set of factors beyond the mere existence of controlling practices.

Another important area explored through the questionnaire survey focused on the use of controlling systems in companies with foreign ownership or capital participation. The underlying assumption guiding this analysis was that companies with international stakeholders would be more likely to implement controlling practices due to the influence of international management standards, compliance requirements, and greater emphasis on financial discipline and strategic oversight.

This assumption was largely confirmed by the results of the survey. Among the companies with foreign participation, the vast majority reported having implemented some form of controlling system. In fact, only 10 companies with foreign ownership indicated that they do not currently utilize controlling tools in their management processes. This relatively small number supports the hypothesis that foreign ownership is a significant factor associated with the adoption of controlling, potentially due to pressure from parent companies, alignment with global best practices, or the necessity of transparent reporting across national boundaries.

The survey also examined the reasons why some companies choose not to implement controlling. The most frequently mentioned explanations reflected both structural and resource-related limitations. Many respondents indicated that they were small firms and therefore did not perceive a strong need for a formal controlling system. Others emphasized that their operations were based exclusively on custom-made or one-off production, where they believed the added value of controlling would be limited.

A number of companies reported a lack of human resources or financial means as the main obstacle, highlighting capacity constraints that prevent them from investing in controlling tools and processes. In some cases, the reluctance stemmed directly from top management, which either showed no interest in implementing controlling or considered financial accounting to be sufficient for managerial decision-making.

Additional reasons included situations where controlling was already secured at the level of the parent company, making local implementation redundant. Some firms also cited cost savings, particularly in terms of avoiding additional personnel expenses. Finally, a small group of respondents mentioned that control activities were already performed through other mechanisms, though in these cases it appeared that the term "controlling" was mistakenly conflated with the narrower concept of "control."

4.1 Analysis of Balance Sheet Items of Companies in Relation to the Implementation of Controlling

4.1.1 Assets Analysis

This section analyzes the values of individual asset categories depending on whether controlling has been implemented in the company or not. A total of 160 companies were analyzed, with data collected through a combination of qualitative and quantitative methods. Qualitative data were obtained via a structured questionnaire survey, while financial data were sourced from a database and subsequently linked to the survey responses.

The analysis focused on 10 key financial asset indicators: total assets, intangible fixed assets, tangible fixed assets, long-term financial assets, total fixed assets, inventories, trade receivables, total receivables, short-term financial assets, and current assets. All financial indicators presented in this section and in subsequent chapters are expressed in thousands CZK.

To evaluate the differences between the two groups (companies with and without implemented controlling), the non-parametric Mann–Whitney U test was employed. This statistical method is suitable for comparing two independent samples when the assumption of normal distribution is not met. The null hypothesis was defined as follows: H_0: $\mu_1 - \mu_2 = 0$, meaning that the medians of the two groups are equal. This hypothesis was tested against the alternative hypothesis H_a: $\mu_1 - \mu_2 \neq 0$. The significance level was set at 0.05.

The results of the statistical testing are summarized in the Table 4.2.

Based on this statistical analysis, it was found that among the monitored asset indicators, only two variables—trade receivables and total receivables—were statistically significant. This indicates a notable difference between companies that have implemented controlling and those that have not, specifically in these two areas. The *p*-values below the 0.05 threshold confirm that the null hypothesis of equal medians must be rejected.

If we represent the results graphically, we find that companies with implemented controlling typically report higher levels of both trade receivables and total receivables. This outcome can be interpreted in several ways. First, companies using controlling often operate within more complex business environments and maintain a broader customer base, which naturally results in larger volumes of receivables. Second, controlling systems may facilitate more accurate tracking and reporting of receivables, leading to greater transparency in financial records.

Additionally, the higher volume of receivables may reflect a strategic focus on invoice-based sales with extended payment terms, which is common in companies with well-established internal structures and processes. However, it is important to note that higher receivables are not always a positive indicator, they may also signal longer cash conversion cycles or weaker customer payment discipline. Therefore, the ability of controlling to assess such risks accurately and support management in working capital decisions is essential.

Table 4.2 Assets analysis in relation to the implementation of controlling

Financial item	Rank sum—Yes[a]	Rank sum—No[b]	U	Z	*p*-value
Total assets	8374	4506	2676	1.1402	0.2542
Intangible fixed assets	3827	1426	898	1.5974	0.1102
Tangible fixed assets	7392	4236	2406	1.3325	0.1827
Financial fixed assets	1408	803	452	0.8858	0.3757
Fixed assets	8390	4490	2660	1.1966	0.2315
Inventories	5961	3630	2220	−0.0681	0.9457
Trade receivables	8766	4114	2284	2.5218	0.0117
Total receivables	9034	3846	2016	3.4664	0.0005
Short-term financial assets	8006	4874	2956	−0.1533	0.8781
Current assets	8246	4634	2804	0.6890	0.4908

[a]Controlling implemented; [b]Controlling not implemented
Source Own processing

Regarding the remaining financial indicators, the statistical analysis shows that there is no statistically significant difference between companies with implemented controlling systems and those without them.

However, when examining the actual values more closely, certain trends can still be observed. For instance, companies that have implemented controlling tend to report higher values in several key financial metrics, even if the differences are not statistically significant. A notable example is the total assets indicator, where companies with controlling in place generally display higher asset values compared to companies without such systems.

This pattern may suggest that controlling is more commonly adopted in larger enterprises with more complex operational structures and greater resource requirements. These organizations often require more robust planning, monitoring, and financial coordination—functions that controlling is specifically designed to support.

From a managerial standpoint, even non-significant differences in key indicators like total assets can carry strategic implications. Higher asset values may reflect stronger investment capacity, broader operational scope, or more diversified business activities. In such contexts, controlling serves as a crucial framework for ensuring these resources are effectively allocated and utilized. It enables better asset management, improved capital budgeting, and more informed strategic decision-making.

4.1.2 Analysis of Liabilities

In this subsection, the values of individual liability items will be analyzed in relation to whether or not controlling has been implemented. A total of 160 companies were analyzed, within which 10 liability-related financial indicators were evaluated (total liabilities, equity, registered capital, retained earnings from previous years, total payables, external capital, long-term payables, trade payables, bank loans and borrowings, and short-term payables).

For the analysis of these indicators, the Mann–Whitney U test was also applied. The null hypothesis was defined as the assumption that the medians of both groups are identical, i.e., $H_0: \mu_1 - \mu_2 = 0$, and was tested against the alternative hypothesis $H_a: \mu_1 - \mu_2 \neq 0$. The statistical significance level was set at 0.05.

The results of the statistical test for these indicators are presented in the Table 4.3.

The results of this statistical analysis show that among the analyzed liability indicators, four indicators proved to be statistically significant: registered capital, total liabilities, debt capital (external sources), and short-term liabilities. Based on these findings, it can be concluded that companies that have implemented controlling systems generally achieve higher values in all of these indicators compared to those that have not.

For visualization purposes, the indicators debt capital (external sources) and short-term liabilities were selected, as they represent two key areas of financial management influenced by controlling activities. Interestingly, when the level of statistical

Table 4.3 Liabilities analysis in relation to the implementation of controlling

Financial item	Rank sum—Yes[a]	Rank sum—No[b]	U	Z	*p*-value
Total liabilities	8350	4530	2700	1.0556	0.2912
Equity	7731	4830	2880	−0.2132	0.8312
Registered capital	7570	4058	2228	2.0035	0.0451
Retained earnings from previous years	6171	4269	2076	−1.4587	0.1446
Total liabilities (external sources)	8830	4050	2220	2.7474	0.0060
Debt capital	8802	4078	2248	2.6487	0.0081
Long-term liabilities	8346	4534	2704	1.0415	0.2976
Trade payables	8578	4302	2472	1.8592	0.0630
Bank loans and borrowings	8063	4498	2668	0.9727	0.3307
Short-term liabilities	8794	4086	2256	2.6205	0.0088

[a]Controlling implemented; [b]Controlling not implemented
Source Own processing

significance was relaxed to 0.10, trade payables would also be included among the statistically significant indicators, further reinforcing the observed pattern.

From a managerial perspective, these findings suggest that companies with implemented controlling tend to rely more on external sources of financing, which may indicate more active and strategic financial management. Such companies are likely to utilize debt financing deliberately to optimize their capital structure and improve return on equity. This approach reflects a higher level of financial sophistication, where controlling plays a critical role in monitoring debt levels, assessing interest costs, and maintaining liquidity stability.

At the same time, a higher share of short-term liabilities may reflect the need for more dynamic working capital management. Controlling in these organizations often provides tools for short-term liquidity planning, monitoring of payment deadlines, and optimization of supplier relationships. Properly implemented, controlling ensures that short-term liabilities do not create financial tension but instead support operational flexibility and efficient cash flow management.

When examining the remaining indicators, the statistical analysis revealed no significant differences between companies with and without controlling. However, a closer look at the distribution of values indicates some interesting patterns. For example, in the case of retained earnings from previous years, the results show the opposite trend—the indicator tends to be higher in companies without implemented controlling compared to those with controlling systems in place.

This finding may seem counterintuitive at first glance, but it could have several explanations. Companies that have not implemented controlling are often smaller, more traditional enterprises that reinvest profits conservatively and may not engage in proactive investment or expansion strategies. On the other hand, firms with controlling systems typically engage in more dynamic financial and investment management, using retained earnings strategically to fund growth initiatives or innovations. This proactive reinvestment may temporarily reduce accumulated retained earnings while strengthening long-term competitiveness.

From a strategic viewpoint, these results highlight the dual role of controlling—not only as a monitoring and reporting mechanism but also as a tool for optimizing the company's financial structure. By improving the management of equity and liabilities, controlling contributes to long-term stability, risk reduction, and enhanced financial performance. The findings confirm that controlling provides measurable benefits in companies where financial planning and risk management are closely integrated with decision-making processes.

4.2 Analysis of Costs, Revenues, Profit, and Cash Flow in Relation to the Implementation of Controlling

The foundation of successful management lies in a comprehensive understanding of the interrelationships between costs, revenues, profit, income, and expenditures. A company's overall performance depends largely on its ability to identify and maintain an optimal structure of outputs and activities within its business processes; one that meets customer expectations while ensuring the highest possible revenues with proportionally low and efficient costs.

In other words, sustainable profitability is achieved when a company effectively balances its value creation for customers and cost efficiency within operations. This requires a systematic approach to planning, monitoring, and evaluating financial flows—areas in which controlling plays a crucial role.

Controlling provides management with the analytical tools necessary to track how costs are generated, how revenues evolve, and how these elements influence profitability and liquidity. Through regular analysis of cost behavior, margin structures, and cash flow dynamics, companies can better understand their internal efficiency, identify financial bottlenecks, and take corrective measures in time.

Furthermore, analyzing the relationships between costs, revenues, profit, and cash flow in connection with the implementation of controlling systems allows organizations to determine whether controlling contributes to greater transparency, improved decision-making, and more stable financial performance. This analysis also highlights how different companies, depending on their level of controlling maturity, translate financial information into actionable strategies that enhance profitability and ensure long-term sustainability.

4.2.1 Analysis of Costs and Revenues in Relation to the Implementation of Controlling

In this next section, the values of individual cost and revenue items from the income statements will be analyzed based on whether or not controlling has been implemented. This time, a total of 142 companies were analyzed, within which 10 indicators of costs and revenues were evaluated: revenue from the sale of goods, cost of goods sold, consumption of materials and energy, operating income, revenue from the sale of own products and services, personnel costs, depreciation of fixed assets, operating expenses, interest expenses, corporate income tax from ordinary activities.

The lower number of companies in this (and other) analyses is due to the fact that some of the companies did not have complete data available in their income statements.

To analyze the indicators, the Mann–Whitney U test was used. The null hypothesis was defined as the assumption that the medians of the two samples are equal (i.e., H_0: $\mu_1 - \mu_2 = 0$), and this was tested against the alternative hypothesis (H_a: $\mu_1 - \mu_2 \neq 0$). Statistical testing was conducted at a significance level of 0.05.

The results of the statistical test for all indicators are presented in the Table 4.4.

Table 4.4 Costs and revenues analysis in relation to the implementation of controlling

Financial item	Rank sum—Yes[a]	Rank sum—No[b]	U	Z	p-value
Revenue from the sale of goods	3303	2157	1254	0.3147	0.7530
Cost of goods sold	8382	4498	2668	1.1684	0.2427
Consumption of materials and energy	5711	2804	1628	1.6378	0.1015
Operating income	8434	4446	2616	1.3517	0.1765
Revenue from the sale of own products and services	8950	3930	2100	3.1703	0.0015
Personnel costs	7091	3062	1684	2.7757	0.0055
Depreciation of fixed assets	6735	3418	2040	1.2682	0.2047
Operating expenses	8450	4430	2600	1.4081	0.1591
Interest expenses	4351	1977	1236	1.0416	0.2976
Corporate income tax from ordinary activities	3939	2847	1164	−2.2375	0.0253

[a]Controlling implemented; [b]Controlling not implemented
Source Own processing

Based on the results of the statistical analysis, three cost and revenue indicators were found to be statistically significant in relation to the implementation of controlling: revenue from the sale of own products and services, personnel costs, corporate income tax from ordinary activities.

The findings suggest that companies with implemented controlling tend to achieve higher values in both revenue from the sale of own products and services and personnel costs. These results indicate a greater ability among controlled firms to manage and optimize operations that directly contribute to revenue generation. At the same time, higher personnel costs may reflect greater investments into human resources, such as hiring qualified staff, training, or performance-based remuneration, often associated with more structured management systems.

On the other hand, for the indicator corporate income tax from ordinary activities, the opposite trend was observed. In this case, companies without implemented controlling reported higher values, which may reflect either a lower ability to optimize tax-related planning or higher taxable profit levels that are not sufficiently balanced by deductions or cost optimization strategies. It may also suggest inefficiencies in tax planning or the absence of forward-looking financial management in companies without a structured controlling system.

For the remaining indicators, the statistical analysis did not confirm a significant difference between companies with and without controlling. However, visual analysis and descriptive statistics reveal that certain trends still emerge. One such example is the indicator depreciation of fixed assets, where values tend to be higher among companies with controlling systems in place.

This may indicate that such companies invest more in long-term assets, such as machinery, technology, or infrastructure, further emphasizing a long-term strategic focus and forward-looking investment behavior that controlling often supports. While these differences may not be statistically significant at the 5% level, they offer relevant managerial insights. Companies using controlling tools may better manage capital investments and asset utilization, which are key elements in sustaining competitiveness.

From a management perspective, these findings underscore the importance of adopting structured controlling practices not only for tracking financial outcomes but also for influencing the strategic allocation of resources, investment decisions, and revenue optimization efforts. The ability to generate higher revenues from core business activities and allocate more resources to personnel development may provide companies with a competitive advantage in both the short and long term.

4.2.2 Analysis of Profitability and Cash Flow in Relation to the Implementation of Controlling

In this next section, the values of various types of profit figures and cash flow will be analyzed in relation to whether or not controlling has been implemented. A total of five different types of profit indicators were evaluated (operating profit, financial profit, earnings before tax (EBT), earnings before interest and tax (EBIT), earnings after tax (EAT)) along with the cash flow indicator.

For the analysis of these indicators, the Mann–Whitney U test was used. The null hypothesis was defined as the assumption that the medians of the two groups are identical, i.e., H_0: $\mu_1 - \mu_2 = 0$, and this was tested against the alternative hypothesis H_a: $\mu_1 - \mu_2 \neq 0$. The statistical significance level was set at 0.05. The results of the statistical test for these indicators are presented in the Table 4.5.

The results of this analysis indicate that statistically significant differences were found only for the indicator financial profit (financial result). Therefore, it can be concluded that companies with implemented controlling systems tend to achieve lower values of financial profit compared to those without controlling.

Although no statistically significant relationships were confirmed for the other profit indicators, a closer look at the graphical visualization reveals that most profitability indicators, such as operating profit, EBIT, and EBT, tend to be higher in companies without controlling implementation. This suggests that, while controlling may not directly translate into immediate profit growth, it may influence the structure and stability of profits rather than their absolute level.

The selected indicators Operating Profit and Earnings Before Interest and Tax (EBIT) illustrate this tendency. Companies without controlling appear to achieve slightly higher short-term profit figures, whereas companies with controlling systems tend to demonstrate more balanced and sustainable financial performance over time. This could indicate that controlling-oriented firms focus on long-term efficiency, optimization, and risk mitigation, rather than short-term profit maximization.

From a managerial perspective, these results highlight an important insight: the implementation of controlling should not be assessed solely through immediate profit indicators. Instead, it serves as a comprehensive management framework that enhances decision-making quality, cost transparency, and long-term financial health.

Table 4.5 Analysis of profitability and cash flow in relation to the implementation of controlling

Financial item	Rank sum—Yes[a]	Rank sum—No[b]	U	Z	*p*-value
Operating profit	7758	5122	2708	−1.0274	0.3042
Financial profit	5915	4238	1820	−2.1998	0.0278
Profit before tax (EBT)	7722	5158	2672	−1.1543	0.2484
Profit before interest and tax (EBIT)	6147	4006	2052	−1.2174	0.2234
Profit after tax (EAT)	6051	4102	1956	−1.6239	0.1044
Cash flow	8106	4774	2944	0.1956	0.8449

[a]Controlling implemented; [b]Controlling not implemented
Source Own processing

Consequently, even though short-term profits may appear lower, such firms may benefit from greater financial resilience and strategic flexibility in the long run.

The differences observed in the analysis of the cash flow indicator were not statistically significant based on the conducted statistical testing. However, the graphical representation of the data suggests that there is a slight, though not substantial, difference between companies with and without implemented controlling systems.

Specifically, it appears that companies with implemented controlling tend to show higher cash flow values compared to those that do not utilize controlling. Although the difference is not large enough to be considered statistically meaningful, it still indicates a positive trend associated with the presence of structured financial and operational control mechanisms.

This observation aligns with the expected outcomes of effective controlling practices, which aim to improve liquidity management, working capital efficiency, and operational cash generation. In this sense, even marginal improvements in cash flow performance can have significant implications for a company's financial stability, investment capacity, and ability to respond to external changes.

Therefore, while the statistical evidence does not confirm a significant impact, the practical implications for financial management and long-term planning suggest that controlling may indeed contribute to healthier and more predictable cash flow development.

4.3 Analysis of Financial Indicators in Relation to the Implementation of Controlling

In this chapter, the financial analysis indicators will be examined in relation to whether or not controlling has been implemented. These indicators were categorized into leverage ratios, liquidity ratios, profitability ratios, and bankruptcy and creditworthiness models. The primary data sources for this analysis were the balance sheets and income statements of the evaluated companies. A total of 142 companies were assessed using statistical analysis, and the Mann–Whitney U test was applied for the evaluation.

4.3.1 Analysis of Leverage Indicators in Relation to the Implementation of Controlling

Leverage indicators provide essential information about a company's financial structure, showing the proportion of assets financed by equity versus debt. These indicators serve as a crucial measure of financial stability, risk exposure, and capital efficiency. While a higher level of indebtedness is often perceived as risky, it is not necessarily negative if it remains within reasonable limits. A moderate degree of leverage can enhance a company's return on equity (ROE) and thereby increase its market value, as borrowed capital can amplify returns when used effectively. However, excessive debt leads to higher interest obligations, lower solvency, and an increased risk of financial distress, particularly during periods of declining profitability or rising interest rates.

In this analysis, several key leverage ratios were evaluated to assess the relationship between financial structure and the implementation of controlling systems. The following indicators were included (Růčková, 2021):

- Total debt ratio—the proportion of total liabilities to total assets, showing overall indebtedness.
- Equity-to-debt ratio—expressing the relationship between own and borrowed capital.
- Interest coverage ratio—measuring the ability of a company to cover its interest expenses from operating profits.
- Credit indebtedness—the share of bank loans and financial assistance in total liabilities.
- Loan repayment period—the average time required to repay outstanding loans.
- Interest rate and interest burden—showing the cost of debt capital and its effect on profitability.
- Equity ratio—indicating the share of equity in total capital, which reflects financial independence.
- Bank loans and borrowings relative to total liabilities—assessing the company's dependence on external financing.

The statistical Mann–Whitney U test was applied to determine whether there were significant differences in leverage indicators between companies with implemented controlling systems and those without. The null hypothesis (H_0) was formulated as follows: the medians of both samples are identical, H_0: $\mu_1 - \mu_2 = 0$. This hypothesis was tested against the alternative hypothesis (H_a) that the medians differ, H_a: $\mu_1 - \mu_2 \neq 0$. The testing was conducted at a significance level of 0.05.

By evaluating leverage in this context, the analysis aims to determine whether controlling contributes to more balanced capital structures and better financial stability. Companies that actively apply controlling are expected to maintain optimal levels of debt, ensuring sufficient financing for growth while avoiding excessive financial risk. Table 4.6 presents the statistical results for the analyzed indicators, providing an empirical basis for understanding the financial implications of controlling implementation.

The statistical analysis revealed that four leverage indicators showed statistically significant differences between companies with and without implemented controlling systems. These indicators include Total Debt Ratio, Equity Debt Ratio, Interest Burden, and Equity-to-Total Capital Ratio.

The results indicate that companies with implemented controlling systems tend to exhibit higher values for Total Debt Ratio, Equity Debt Ratio, and Interest Burden. This suggests that these companies rely more heavily on external financing and may take on higher levels of debt to support investment and growth initiatives. At the same

Table 4.6 Analysis of leverage indicators in relation to the implementation of controlling

Financial item	Rank sum—Yes[a]	Rank sum—No[b]	U	Z	*p*-value
Total debt ratio (%)	9196	3684	1854	4.0374	0.0001
Equity debt ratio (%)	9132	3748	1918	3.8118	0.0001
Interest coverage	7860	5020	2810	−0.6679	0.5042
Credit indebtedness (%)	8342	4538	2708	1.0274	0.3042
Loan repayment period (years)	8182	4698	2868	0.4635	0.6430
Interest rate (%)	8108	4772	2942	0.2027	0.8394
Interest burden (%)	8644	4236	2406	2.0918	0.0365
Equity-to-total capital ratio (%)	6904	5976	1854	−4.0374	0.0001
Bank loans and borrowings (% of liabilities)	8224	4656	2826	0.6115	0.5409

[a]Controlling implemented; [b]Controlling not implemented
Source Own processing

time, controlling likely enables them to manage this debt more effectively through systematic monitoring, cost optimization, and strategic financial planning.

Conversely, the indicator Equity-to-Total Capital Ratio demonstrates an opposite trend; it is higher in companies without controlling. This may imply that firms lacking formal controlling systems prefer more conservative financing structures, relying predominantly on equity to avoid financial risk. However, such firms might also be missing opportunities to leverage external financing for expansion and value creation.

For the indicators Interest Coverage and Loan Repayment Period, the results were inconclusive, even when assessed through graphical visualization. This ambiguity could be due to varying debt structures, interest rate policies, or the limited sample size of companies with detailed loan data.

Among the remaining indicators, although statistical significance was not confirmed, graphical analysis revealed additional insights. Specifically, the indicators Credit Indebtedness and Bank Loans and Borrowings tend to be higher in companies with controlling, indicating that these firms may use borrowed funds more strategically as part of their financial management framework. In contrast, the Interest Rate indicator showed higher values in companies without controlling, suggesting that firms lacking structured financial control might face less favorable credit conditions, for example, higher interest rates due to weaker credit ratings or less efficient financial planning.

Overall, the analysis implies that the implementation of controlling is associated with a more active approach to financial management, including a greater use of external financing. However, this also requires stronger risk monitoring and liquidity management to prevent over-leverage. These findings highlight the dual role of controlling: while it enables companies to pursue growth through strategic financing, it also demands robust systems to safeguard financial stability.

4.3.2 Analysis of Liquidity Indicators in Relation to the Implementation of Controlling

Liquidity can be defined as the extent to which a company is able to convert its assets into cash and use these funds to cover its due liabilities. In other words, liquidity expresses the company's ability to meet its financial obligations as they come due. Liquidity ratios are relative indicators that show the degree to which a company is capable of paying its short-term debts. The main sources of data for calculating these ratios are the income statement, balance sheet, and the accompanying notes to the financial statements.

The current ratio is calculated by dividing total current assets by short-term liabilities. The optimal value of the current ratio is typically between 1.8 and 2.5, indicating how many times the company can cover all its short-term obligations with its current assets.

The quick ratio is computed similarly to the current ratio, but inventories are subtracted from current assets in the numerator. Its recommended value ranges between 1.0 and 1.5.

The cash ratio (or immediate liquidity) measures the proportion of financial assets to short-term liabilities, and its value should lie between 0.2 and 0.5 (Růčková, 2021).

Within the analysis of liquidity indicators, four specific ratios were evaluated: the current ratio, quick ratio, cash ratio, and cash flow liquidity (expressed in percentage terms). The statistical evaluation employed the Mann–Whitney U test, where the null hypothesis (H_0) stated that the medians of the two samples are identical (H_0: $\mu_1 - \mu_2 = 0$), and the alternative hypothesis (H_a) assumed that the medians differ (H_a: $\mu_1 - \mu_2 \neq 0$). The testing was conducted at a significance level of 0.05.

Table 4.7 presents the results of the statistical test for these liquidity indicators.

Table 4.7 Analysis of liquidity indicators in relation to the implementation of controlling

Financial item	Rank sum—Yes[a]	Rank sum—No[b]	U	Z	*p*-value
Current ratio	6830	6050	1780	−4.2982	0.0000
Quick ratio	7538	5342	2488	−1.8028	0.0714
Cash ratio	7144	5736	2094	−3.1915	0.0014
Cash flow liquidity ratio (in %)	6932	5948	1882	−3.9387	0.0001

[a]Controlling implemented; [b]Controlling not implemented
Source Own processing

Based on the results presented in the table above, it can be observed that the indicators of current liquidity, immediate liquidity, and cash flow liquidity show statistically significant differences in their values between companies that have implemented controlling systems and those that have not. These differences were confirmed at the previously mentioned significance level of 0.05.

If the significance threshold were relaxed to 0.10, all analyzed liquidity indicators would exhibit statistically significant differences. This suggests that the presence of a controlling system may have a measurable influence on the company's ability to manage liquidity and meet its short-term obligations.

From a visual perspective, the graphical representation of the results shows that, in terms of current liquidity, quick liquidity (although this indicator did not reach statistical significance at the 0.05 level), and immediate liquidity, companies without controlling tend to achieve higher liquidity values than those that have implemented controlling. This pattern may indicate a more conservative approach to asset management in companies lacking formal controlling structures, whereas firms with controlling may operate with tighter liquidity in pursuit of greater efficiency in capital utilization.

4.3.3 Analysis of Profitability Indicators

Profitability represents the company's ability to generate profit in relation to various evaluated criteria. It is one of the fundamental measures of business performance, expressing the firm's capacity to create new resources, namely to generate profit through the effective use of invested capital.

Profitability indicators are ratio measures (expressed as percentages), where profit appears in the numerator and the corresponding base variable in the denominator. These ratios provide insight into how efficiently a company utilizes its resources to achieve profit.

Within the analysis of profitability indicators, five specific measures were evaluated: Return on equity (ROE), Return on assets (ROA), Return on long-term capital, Return on sales (ROS), and Return on costs (ROC).

The Mann–Whitney U test was applied for statistical evaluation. The null hypothesis (H_0) stated that the medians of the two samples are identical (H_0: $\mu_1 - \mu_2 = 0$), while the alternative hypothesis (H_a) assumed that the medians differ (H_a: $\mu_1 - \mu_2 \neq 0$). Statistical testing was conducted at a significance level of 0.05.

Table 4.8 presents the results of the statistical test for these profitability indicators.

Based on the results presented in the table above, it can be concluded that the indicators of return on assets (ROA), return on sales (ROS), and return on costs exhibit statistically significant differences between companies that have implemented controlling systems and those that have not.

More specifically, it was found that companies without an established controlling system show a higher median for these profitability indicators compared to those that have controlling in place. This finding suggests that the existence of a controlling

Table 4.8 Analysis of profitability indicators in relation to the implementation of controlling

Financial item	Rank sum—Yes[a]	Rank sum—No[b]	U	Z	p-value
Return on equity (ROE)	6731	3422	2044	1.2513	0.2108
Return on assets (ROA)	5933	4220	1838	−2.1236	0.0337
Return on long-term capital	6535	3618	2240	0.4213	0.6735
Return on sales (ROS)	5923	4230	1828	−2.1659	0.0303
Return on costs (ROC)	5967	4186	1872	−1.9796	0.0477

[a]Controlling implemented; [b]Controlling not implemented
Source Own processing

function may influence profitability outcomes, potentially as a result of stricter cost management, more conservative investment policies, or a stronger focus on long-term stability rather than short-term profit maximization.

From a managerial perspective, these results provide important insights into the role of controlling within the enterprise. Controlling is not primarily aimed at maximizing short-term profitability but rather at ensuring effective coordination, transparency, and sustainability in financial and operational decision-making. Companies that have implemented controlling often prioritize process optimization, cost control, and risk management, which can lead to lower but more stable profitability levels. In contrast, enterprises operating without formal controlling structures may achieve temporarily higher profitability due to greater operational flexibility and less rigorous budgetary discipline, though this can come at the expense of long-term efficiency and stability.

From a management control viewpoint, these findings highlight the importance of balancing profitability performance with strategic control mechanisms. The implementation of controlling can thus be interpreted not as a constraint on profitability but as an investment in organizational resilience, data-driven decision-making, and sustainable financial performance.

4.3.4 Analysis of Bankruptcy and Creditworthiness Models

Bankruptcy models are based on the company's asset and capital structure. They function as early warning systems, as the behavior of selected financial indicators can signal potential threats to a firm's financial health (Kislingerová, 2007). Such models are widely used in financial management and corporate governance to identify companies at risk of financial distress before severe liquidity or solvency problems occur.

Within the analysis of bankruptcy and creditworthiness indicators, three models were evaluated: the Taffler model, the IN99 Index, and the Quick Test.

The Taffler model is a bankruptcy prediction model that estimates the probability of corporate failure based on a combination of financial ratios. It is particularly valued for its ability to differentiate between financially healthy and distressed firms with relatively high accuracy.

The IN99 Index is a creditworthiness (bonity) model constructed from the owner's perspective. It serves as an indicator of value creation, especially in situations where the market price of shares does not provide reliable information or where the cost of equity cannot be determined precisely. Thus, the IN99 Index can be used as a proxy for assessing the company's performance and potential to generate shareholder value in privately held or non-listed firms.

The Quick Test provides information on whether a company is over-indebted or financially balanced. The model was designed to minimize the influence of external or random factors and includes four key analytical areas: stability, liquidity, profitability, and overall financial performance. This multi-dimensional approach ensures a comprehensive assessment of both the company's financial stability and its profitability position, thus allowing managers to evaluate the overall financial soundness of the enterprise (Růčková, 2021).

For the statistical evaluation, the Mann–Whitney U test was employed. The null hypothesis (H_0) stated that the medians of both samples are identical (H_0: $\mu_1 - \mu_2 = 0$), while the alternative hypothesis (H_a) proposed that the medians differ (H_a: $\mu_1 - \mu_2 \neq 0$). Statistical testing was conducted at a significance level of 0.05.

Table 4.9 presents the results of the statistical test for the analyzed bankruptcy and creditworthiness models.

Based on the results presented in the table above, it can be concluded that the indicator derived from the Taffler model shows statistically significant differences in values between companies that have implemented controlling systems and those that have not.

Table 4.9 Analysis of bankruptcy and creditworthiness models in relation to the implementation of controlling

Bankruptcy and creditworthiness model	Rank sum—Yes[a]	Rank sum—No[b]	U	Z	*p*-value
Tafflerův model	5565	4588	1470	−3.6819	0.0002
Index IN99	6235	3918	2140	−0.8448	0.3982
Quick test	6705	3448	2070	1.1412	0.2538

[a]Controlling implemented; [b]Controlling not implemented
Source Own processing

The graphical representation further reveals that enterprises without controlling display a higher median of the Taffler score compared to those with controlling. According to the model's interpretation:

$T > 0.3$—low probability of corporate bankruptcy,
$0.2 < T < 0.3$—grey zone of indeterminate results,
$T < 0.2$—increased probability of bankruptcy.

In simplified terms, the higher the value of the Taffler indicator, the lower the probability of corporate failure. This finding suggests that companies without a formal controlling system, at least according to this model, appear to be in a stronger financial position or show lower bankruptcy risk.

However, when analyzing the graphical results for the IN99 Index and the Quick Test, it becomes evident that although these indicators did not show statistically significant differences, they exhibit opposite tendencies compared to the Taffler model.

The IN99 Index is interpreted as follows:

$IN99 > 2.07$—the company creates new value for the owner,
$1.42 \leq IN99 < 2.07$—the company rather creates value for the owner,
$1.089 \leq IN99 < 1.42$—it is not clear whether the company creates or does not create value,
$0.684 \leq IN99 < 1.089$—the company rather does not create value,
$IN99 < 0.684$—the company does not create value for the owner.

Thus, the higher the IN99 Index, the greater the value creation for the owner. In this case, the median IN99 value is higher for companies without controlling, whereas for the Quick Test, the median is higher in companies with controlling. According to Kralicek (1993), a Quick Test score below 2 indicates a very good financial situation, while a score above 3 suggests poor financial health.

From a managerial and controlling perspective, these results offer several important insights. The fact that companies without controlling tend to achieve higher median values of the Taffler and IN99 indicators may reflect a greater short-term profitability and operational flexibility due to less formalized control mechanisms. Such firms may be more opportunistic, pursuing short-term gains without the constraints of systematic planning and monitoring.

Conversely, companies with established controlling systems often emphasize strategic stability, cost optimization, and long-term financial sustainability. The implementation of controlling typically introduces a more disciplined approach to resource allocation, performance monitoring, and risk management. While this can lead to slightly lower profitability or solvency ratios in the short term, it contributes to greater transparency, improved decision-making, and long-term resilience.

In terms of managerial implications, the findings suggest that controlling should not be evaluated solely by its immediate financial outcomes, but rather by its strategic contribution to sustainable business management. Although the models indicate stronger financial metrics in companies without controlling, this may also imply a higher exposure to financial risks and a lack of early warning mechanisms that controlling provides.

In conclusion, when viewed through the lens of bankruptcy and creditworthiness models, companies without controlling currently exhibit stronger financial indicators. However, from the standpoint of managerial control and corporate governance, companies with controlling benefit from enhanced risk management, predictability, and long-term stability—factors that may not be immediately visible in traditional financial ratios but are critical for sustainable performance.

4.4 Analysis of Operational and Strategic Controlling

For company management, it is essential to use various controlling methods and tools that are necessary for evaluating the performance and efficiency of economic processes. An important aspect is the effect and benefits these tools bring to the enterprise.

As part of the analysis of operational and strategic controlling, data were obtained from a questionnaire survey conducted among 245 companies. Of this sample, 103 companies did not have controlling implemented, while 142 companies had an established controlling system.

In the following section, which focuses on the analysis of operational and strategic controlling tools, only companies that have implemented controlling as an instrument of internal management will be analyzed. The number of analyzed companies may be slightly lower due to the fact that some respondents did not answer all questions in the survey.

Among these companies, 17% were engaged in trade, 28% in service provision, 45% in manufacturing, and 10% operated in both manufacturing and trade. Regarding company ownership, 77% of the enterprises had no foreign participation, while 23% had foreign ownership participation.

4.4.1 Analysis of Operational Controlling Tools

Within the scope of operational controlling tools, the following areas were examined:

- Integration of controlling into the company's organizational structure,
- Circular system of managerial accounting,
- Preparation of operational plans,
- Cost classification into direct and overhead, direct and indirect, variable and fixed costs,
- Costing methods used,
- Types of costing formulas,
- Methods applied for the allocation of indirect costs,

- Use of performance-based depreciation within controlling (managerial accounting),
- Types of variances analyzed,
- Frequency of variance evaluation,
- Preparation of internal company reports.

Integration of Controlling into the Organizational Structure of the Company

A fundamental issue in the organization of controlling concerns whether a company chooses to rely on the work of an external controller (external controlling) or to implement an internal controlling function, and if so, whether this function will operate with or without a designated controller. Closely related to this question is the decision regarding whether controlling will be integrated into the company's organizational structure as a line or staff function.

External controlling is primarily used by smaller enterprises, for which it would be financially demanding to maintain a full-time controller position within their structure. For this reason, the following analysis focuses more closely on external controlling and examines the size of companies (in terms of number of employees) that utilize such services. The results show that only about 14% of companies use external controlling, and among these, 79% are small enterprises with up to 49 employees.

The most common form of integration is controlling established as a staff department, present in 36% of companies. When controlling operates as a staff function, it typically has no formal decision-making authority and cannot issue binding instructions to line management. Its characteristic roles include preparing managerial decisions, coordinating partial plans, and supervising the implementation of adopted measures. This structure positions controlling primarily as an advisory and analytical function, supporting management with relevant information, forecasts, and performance evaluations rather than enforcing decisions directly.

Approximately 26% of companies integrate controlling as a line function. A line position of controlling is particularly suitable for small enterprises or in crisis situations, where rapid and authoritative decision-making is required. In this configuration, controlling assumes greater responsibility and accountability for its decisions, holding both decision-making and directive powers. This structure allows the controller to directly influence operational management, which can enhance responsiveness and implementation speed but may also blur the boundary between management execution and management support.

The choice between line and staff integration of controlling thus depends largely on how top management perceives the role of controlling; whether it views it as a supportive, advisory function or as an executive instrument of management control.

A combination of line and staff approaches appears in 25% of companies. This hybrid model enables collaboration between line managers and the controlling department, where management is executed both from the technical/professional side (ensured by controlling) and the performance/execution side (ensured by line managers). In this structure, the controlling department obtains limited directive authority, conditional on joint decision-making with line management in predefined situations. This cooperation fosters a balanced distribution of competencies and enhances the integration of controlling into the overall managerial decision-making process.

From a managerial perspective, the way controlling is embedded within the organizational structure significantly affects its influence on business performance, decision-making processes, and communication flow. A staff-based controlling structure supports analytical precision, neutrality, and long-term strategic oversight, while a line-based structure strengthens operational effectiveness, agility, and accountability. The hybrid approach, combining both, can be viewed as an optimal compromise, ensuring both strategic alignment and operational implementation.

In conclusion, the organizational positioning of controlling reflects the management philosophy and culture of the enterprise. Firms that integrate controlling as an active line function tend to emphasize management control and accountability, whereas those employing it as a staff function highlight support, coordination, and information-based decision-making. The chosen approach therefore directly influences the efficiency of managerial processes, quality of decisions, and overall adaptability of the company to changing market conditions (Table 4.10).

We can therefore conclude that the higher the hierarchical level of controlling within the organizational structure, the greater its effectiveness and impact on overall business management. From a managerial point of view, positioning the controller function at the top management level allows for better coordination, direct access to strategic information, and stronger influence on key decision-making processes. Consequently, it is often recommended that the controller's role be established as high as possible in the organizational hierarchy to ensure the effective integration of controlling into corporate management and strategic planning.

Table 4.10 Integration of controlling into the organizational structure of the company

Integration of controlling into the organizational structure of the company	% of total number
External controlling	13.57
– number of employees 0–9	26.32
– number of employees 10–49	52.63
– number of employees 50–99	0
– number of employees 100–249	10.53
– number of employees 250–499	10.53
Controlling organized as a line function	25.71
Controlling organized as a staff function	35.71
A hybrid (line–staff) controlling structure	25

Source Own processing

However, this organizational arrangement also brings certain practical and ethical challenges. When the controller participates directly in decision-making processes, they may later be required to evaluate and assess the consequences of their own decisions, which can compromise the objectivity and independence of the controlling function. This dual role, being both a participant in decision-making and an evaluator of decisions, creates potential conflicts of interest and may undermine the credibility of controlling reports and analyses.

For this reason, many organizations find it more appropriate to position the controlling department at the second managerial level. This structural arrangement ensures effective vertical communication with top management while maintaining sufficient independence and neutrality in evaluating performance and financial outcomes. At the same time, it allows for horizontal integration with other departments, fostering collaboration and information flow across the organization.

From a managerial governance perspective, placing controlling at the second level creates a balance between authority and objectivity—it provides controllers with the proximity needed to influence management decisions while safeguarding their analytical independence. This positioning thus strengthens the coordination role of controlling, enhances transparency in management processes, and supports evidence-based decision-making across the enterprise.

One-Circle and Two-Circle Systems in Internal Accounting

This section analyzes a total of 132 companies regarding the structure of their managerial accounting systems. In the development of corporate information systems, two primary approaches are used to organize the relationship between financial accounting and managerial accounting: the one-circle system and the two-circle system of accounting information.

The two-circle system is characterized by the coexistence of two relatively independent accounting subsystems (financial accounting and managerial accounting) each serving different reporting and decision-making purposes. These two systems are linked through interface accounts and difference accounts. Interface accounts capture information recorded in financial accounting that also needs to be reflected in managerial accounting, ensuring data consistency and traceability. This setup provides a more robust and adaptable system for internal control, budgeting, and performance measurement.

As the analysis shows, the two-circle system is more commonly used by companies with 50 or more employees. Larger firms typically have more complex operational and organizational structures, making it necessary to separate internal and external reporting for both efficiency and compliance purposes. This separation allows controlling departments to create customized internal reports that support strategic decision-making, cost management, and performance evaluation without being constrained by the formats and principles of external financial reporting.

In contrast, the one-circle system is more prevalent among smaller companies with fewer than 50 employees. In this system, the varying information needs of users are addressed within the same accounting framework using detailed analytical records and difference accounts. While less flexible than the two-circle model, it is more cost-effective and less resource-intensive, which suits the needs of small and micro-enterprises.

Interestingly, a hybrid approach, combining features of both systems, is most frequently adopted by companies with 10 to 49 employees. These organizations are often in transition—too large for purely one-circle systems, yet not large enough to justify full separation—and benefit from a pragmatic blend of both methods to meet their reporting and control needs.

From the perspective of industry type, the two-circle system and hybrid models are most commonly used by manufacturing firms (27.27%), followed by service companies (16.67%) and trading companies (10.61%). This finding suggests that industries with complex production processes and internal cost structures, such as manufacturing, have a greater need for comprehensive internal reporting and thus benefit more from the two-circle approach.

Furthermore, the data reveals that none of the companies with 250 or more employees use a one-circle system. This underscores the fact that as company size and complexity increase, the need for differentiated and specialized accounting systems becomes essential. Larger organizations require detailed managerial reports that go beyond the capabilities of a one-circle system and support advanced functions such as strategic planning, cost control, and performance optimization.

The structure of accounting systems has significant implications for the quality and effectiveness of the controlling function. Companies using the two-circle system are generally better positioned to leverage controlling as a strategic management tool. This is because such systems allow for the development of customized internal reports, cost center tracking, variance analysis, and real-time performance monitoring. The separation of financial and managerial data enables controllers to focus more on forward-looking analyses and value creation, rather than simply replicating financial accounting outputs.

In contrast, companies relying on a one-circle system may face limitations in their ability to implement advanced controlling tools. These firms often struggle with data granularity and flexibility, which may hinder the implementation of activity-based costing, target costing, or strategic performance indicators such as KPIs aligned with balanced scorecards or strategic maps.

The results of this analysis highlight the need for companies to reassess their information systems and consider transitioning toward a two-circle or hybrid accounting model. Doing so would enable more sophisticated controlling practices, thereby enhancing decision-making, supporting strategic planning, and contributing to overall organizational performance.

As controlling becomes an increasingly critical function in a competitive and data-driven business environment, the ability to integrate financial accuracy with managerial insight will become a key differentiator. Therefore, the choice of accounting system structure should not be seen merely as a technical or administrative decision, but rather as a strategic enabler of effective management and sustainable growth..

Preparation of Operational Plans

An essential component of operational controlling tools is the preparation of operational plans and budgets. These plans may cover various time periods, depending primarily on the nature of the company's activities and its size. Smaller enterprises with simpler product structures or homogeneous production processes tend to create operational plans for longer periods, as their activities are often more predictable and less complex. In contrast, larger enterprises with more complex and diverse product portfolios typically develop shorter planning cycles to allow for greater flexibility and responsiveness to market changes.

As part of the empirical survey, the frequency of operational planning was analyzed based on company size measured by the number of employees. According to the findings summarized in the following table, the most common planning horizon is one year (used by 45% of companies), followed by quarterly planning (30%). On the other hand, planning on a semi-annual basis is the least used, mostly by microenterprises with fewer than nine employees.

From a segmentation perspective, based on company size, both the table and the subsequent chart reveal important patterns. Small businesses with fewer than 49 employees most frequently prepare annual operational plans. Quarterly planning is dominant among medium-sized companies with 50–99 employees, while monthly or even shorter planning intervals are most commonly used by firms with 100–249 employees. This differentiation indicates a clear relationship between organizational complexity and the need for more frequent performance monitoring and resource allocation.

The frequency and structure of operational planning have direct implications for the effectiveness of the controlling function and the overall management system. In smaller companies, the preference for annual planning often reflects a more stable operational environment and limited resources dedicated to planning activities. However, this can pose a risk if the external environment changes rapidly, as these businesses may lack the agility to adjust in time.

In contrast, more frequent planning cycles in larger companies reflect a higher degree of organizational complexity and the need for tighter control over operations. Monthly or short-term planning enables these firms to detect deviations early, respond more quickly to unexpected changes, and fine-tune their resource allocation in real time. This is particularly important for manufacturing firms with high fixed costs or service firms that rely heavily on workforce planning and utilization.

For controllers, the planning frequency determines the depth and granularity of data collection and analysis. Shorter planning cycles require more robust systems for data acquisition, real-time monitoring, forecasting, and scenario analysis. As a result, controllers in larger firms play a more active role in cross-functional coordination, variance analysis, and performance reporting, all of which are essential for informed decision-making.

Moreover, this finding highlights the importance of adapting the controlling function to the size and complexity of the organization. While annual planning may be sufficient for some small enterprises, growing businesses should consider transitioning to shorter planning intervals as part of their scalability strategy. Implementing more frequent and structured planning processes can improve cost control, profitability forecasting, and strategic alignment, ultimately enhancing competitiveness.

In conclusion, the results of this survey suggest that the integration of controlling into the operational planning process must be tailored to organizational characteristics, including size, industry, and product complexity. Companies that effectively align their planning frequency with their operational needs are better positioned to achieve transparency, improve flexibility, and drive strategic performance (Table 4.11).

In terms of company size based on the number of employees, a clear pattern emerges from both the previously mentioned table and the following graph. Small enterprises with up to 49 employees most frequently prepare operational plans for a one-year period. In contrast, quarterly plans are most commonly used by companies with 50–99 employees. Monthly or even shorter planning periods are primarily employed by medium-sized enterprises with 100–249 employees.

This distribution highlights a key trend in operational planning: the complexity and frequency of planning tend to increase with company size. Smaller companies, often with more stable and less complex operations, can afford longer planning horizons without sacrificing responsiveness. On the other hand, larger organizations—especially those with diverse product portfolios or more dynamic markets—require more frequent updates to maintain agility and alignment with strategic goals.

From a controlling perspective, this differentiation has significant implications. In smaller firms, controllers may focus on high-level budgeting and basic variance analysis over longer periods. In medium-sized enterprises, however, controllers are likely to be more involved in continuous monitoring, short-term forecasting, and rolling budgets, ensuring tighter cost control and timely corrective actions. This requires not only robust data systems but also close collaboration with operational managers to align resource planning with market developments.

Ultimately, this insight underlines the importance of tailoring the controlling function and tools to the size and complexity of the organization, ensuring that operational plans serve as a reliable foundation for performance management and decision-making (Fig. 4.4).

Table 4.11 Frequency of preparation of operational plans

Period/Number of employees	0–9 (%)	10–49 (%)	50–99 (%)	100–249 (%)	250–499 (%)	Total (%)
1 Year	50.00	37.50	40.00	55.00	100.00	45.45
6 Months	25.00	7.50	0.00	5.00	0.00	6.49
3 Months	25.00	35.00	50.00	15.00	0.00	29.87
1 Month or less	0.00	20.00	10.00	25.00	0.00	18.18

Source Own processing

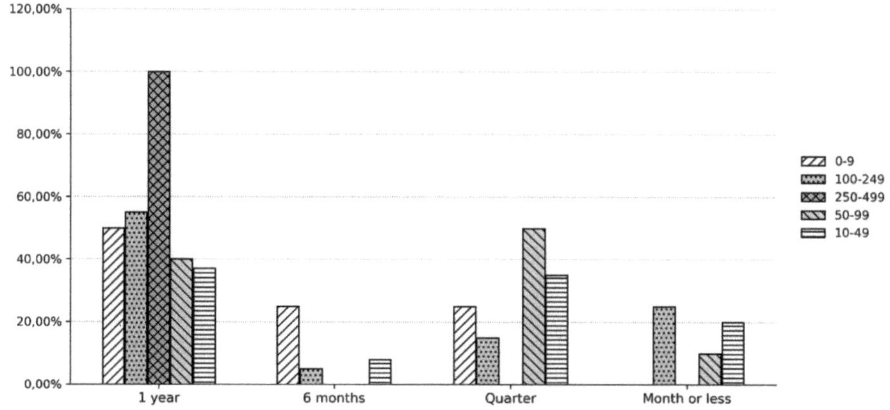

Fig. 4.4 Preparation of operational plans according to the size of the company. *Source* Own processing

Classification of Costs into Direct and Indirect, Variable and Fixed

The classification of costs represents one of the fundamental prerequisites for cost calculation and budgeting. As described in the theoretical part, costs can be categorized from several perspectives. The most common classifications include the division into direct and indirect, prime and overhead, and variable and fixed costs, as well as various combinations of these categories.

The analysis examined which type of cost classification is most frequently used among different types of enterprises and how this classification varies according to company size, measured by the number of employees.

For micro-enterprises (0–9 employees), the most common classification of costs is into prime and overhead (40%). In the group of small enterprises (10–49 employees), costs are most often divided into direct and indirect (29.73%), followed by prime and overhead (21.62%). For medium-small enterprises (50–99 employees), the classification into variable and fixed costs is the most dominant (50%), while the direct and indirect division remains significant (30%). Companies with 100–249 employees also primarily classify costs as variable and fixed (42.86%), with an additional 28.57% combining variable/fixed and direct/indirect perspectives.

In the group of larger medium-sized companies (250–499 employees), only two classifications are present: direct and indirect (66.67%) and a combination of all three types (33.33%).

Overall, across all analyzed enterprises, the most frequent classifications are variable and fixed costs (26.09%) and direct and indirect costs (24.64%). These classifications form the foundation of most costing formulas and methodologies. For instance, the traditional costing formula is built upon direct and indirect costs, while the retrograde costing formula is based on the variable and fixed cost distinction.

When analyzing by industry type, commercial, manufacturing, and service companies most frequently classify costs as variable and fixed (ranging between 21–33%), followed by direct and indirect (21–25%). Enterprises that combine manufacturing and trading activities most commonly apply direct and indirect classification (33.33%). It is also noteworthy that nearly 12% of the surveyed companies do not perform cost classification at all, with the smallest share of such cases occurring among manufacturing firms.

From a controlling perspective, the results of this analysis are crucial for understanding how companies structure their internal cost information, which directly affects the accuracy of budgeting, variance analysis, and decision-making. The predominance of variable and fixed cost classification among larger companies suggests a growing emphasis on cost behavior analysis and break-even management, both of which are essential for dynamic financial control.

In contrast, smaller enterprises that focus mainly on direct and indirect cost classification often rely on simpler accounting structures and traditional costing systems, which are sufficient for short-term operational decisions but may limit deeper strategic insights. For these firms, introducing at least a partial variable/fixed cost perspective could improve their ability to perform flexible budgeting, cost-volume-profit analysis, and scenario modeling.

For management, the type of cost classification determines how effectively the company can allocate resources, set prices, and assess profitability across products or services. Using variable and fixed cost structures supports strategic decision-making, especially under fluctuating market conditions, while direct and indirect classifications are more suitable for production control and cost tracing.

Overall, the findings highlight the necessity of aligning the company's cost accounting structure with its management control system. Enterprises that adapt their cost classification to reflect their strategic objectives gain better tools for performance monitoring, forecasting, and strategic planning, key pillars of effective controlling practice.

Applied Costing Methods and Types of Costing Formulas

The next part of the analysis focused on the types of cost calculations used by companies, divided into preliminary, ongoing, final, and price calculations, as well as their combinations. The findings show that most companies prepare only price calculations (26%), followed by a combination of all types of calculations (17%) and a combination of preliminary, final, and price calculations (16%).

When excluding mixed approaches, the most commonly used calculation type across all enterprises is price calculation (36%), followed by final (25%), preliminary (20%), and ongoing calculations (19%).

When analyzed by type of business, manufacturing firms most frequently use price calculations (22%) and the combination of preliminary, final, and price calculations (16%). Service companies most often employ price calculations as well (37%) and the combination of all four calculation types (26%). In trading companies, price calculations dominate again (33%), while enterprises that are both manufacturing and trading show only marginal results.

The analysis of types of costing formulas was carried out in two dimensions—the retrograde costing formula and the traditional costing formula.

The retrograde costing formula has the following structure:

$$Revenues - Variable\ Costs - Fixed\ Costs = Profit$$

This formula requires that costs be divided into variable and fixed, which makes it more demanding in terms of data reporting and analysis. Consequently, only about 22% of companies use this method.

In contrast, the traditional costing formula, which divides costs into direct and indirect categories, is used by more than 78% of companies. Its structure typically consists of:

$$Direct\ Material + Direct\ Labor + Other\ Direct\ Costs + Manufacturing\ Overhead \\ + Administrative\ Overhead + Selling\ Overhead$$

When analyzing the type of costing formula by enterprise type, both formulas are used most frequently in manufacturing companies—46.67% of these use the retrograde formula, and 46.30% the traditional one.

From a controlling perspective, these findings illustrate the prevailing orientation of enterprises toward traditional cost calculation methods, which rely on direct and indirect cost classification. This approach supports short-term cost control and price setting, but it often lacks the flexibility and analytical depth required for strategic decision-making and performance management.

The low adoption rate of the retrograde costing formula highlights a gap in the application of modern management accounting tools that integrate cost behavior analysis. The retrograde formula, built on the separation of variable and fixed costs, allows for more dynamic profit planning, break-even analysis, and scenario forecasting, which are essential components of advanced controlling systems.

For management, the predominance of price-oriented and traditional costing methods implies a focus on operational efficiency and pricing policy, rather than on long-term strategic management. While price calculations are crucial for competitiveness and margin control, the integration of retrograde or mixed costing models could enhance the company's ability to evaluate profitability under changing market conditions, optimize resource allocation, and support decision-making at different managerial levels.

From a controlling system design standpoint, this analysis suggests that companies should gradually evolve toward hybrid costing models combining both traditional and retrograde principles. Such systems would enable a more accurate understanding of cost structures, facilitate target costing, and strengthen budgetary control by linking operational and strategic perspectives.

Ultimately, the alignment of costing methods with the company's management control framework enhances not only financial transparency but also organizational adaptability and competitiveness in dynamic market environments.

Methods Used for Allocating Indirect Costs

Closely related to costing methods are the techniques used for allocating indirect costs. In this research, the most common methods of indirect cost allocation were analyzed, including:

- The simple division method,
- The division method using ratio numbers,
- The surcharge (overhead rate) method, and
- The Activity-Based Costing (ABC) method, which is based on specific activities and processes.

The results revealed notable differences depending on both the type of enterprise and company size, measured by the number of employees.

Commercial and manufacturing enterprises most frequently use the division method with ratio numbers, while service companies and enterprises that are both manufacturing and commercial most often apply the simple division method, which is the easiest to implement.

Interesting findings emerged regarding the use of the ABC method. Although it is a modern and analytically demanding approach that requires detailed data collection, nearly one-third of service companies reported using it. In contrast, manufacturing firms apply the ABC method the least. This is particularly surprising given that these firms typically face the highest demands for accurate cost allocation, especially in heterogeneous production environments divided into several phases or levels.

The surcharge (overhead rate) method, on the other hand, is increasingly considered outdated and unsuitable for today's complex and dynamic business environment. Nevertheless, it remains in use by approximately one-quarter of the surveyed companies. However, the research clearly shows that none of the larger enterprises (with more than 99 employees) apply this method, indicating that it is used primarily by smaller firms with less sophisticated management accounting systems.

From a controlling and management accounting perspective, these findings highlight the divergent levels of maturity in cost allocation practices among companies of different sizes and industries.

Smaller enterprises tend to rely on simplified allocation methods (such as simple division or ratio division), which are easy to apply but provide only limited accuracy in cost tracking. This can lead to distorted product or service profitability analyses and weakened decision-making foundations. For such firms, the gradual introduction of more advanced approaches (especially ABC) could significantly enhance the transparency of overhead cost behavior, enabling more precise budgeting, pricing, and cost control.

In contrast, larger and more structurally complex companies require data-driven and process-oriented allocation systems to support their controlling functions. The ABC method, despite its higher implementation cost, provides a richer analytical foundation by linking indirect costs directly to activities and processes that consume resources. This alignment strengthens strategic cost management, performance measurement, and value-based decision-making, key pillars of modern controlling systems.

For management, the choice of allocation method directly affects how well cost information reflects operational reality. A company relying on outdated surcharge methods may struggle with inaccurate product costing, leading to pricing errors, inefficient resource allocation, and strategic blind spots. On the other hand, firms adopting ABC or hybrid allocation approaches gain greater control over overheads, the ability to identify non-value-adding activities, and improved insight into process efficiency.

Overall, the study's findings confirm that cost allocation methods are not merely accounting techniques, but strategic tools that influence managerial control and corporate performance. Enterprises that modernize their cost allocation systems strengthen their controlling effectiveness, decision relevance, and long-term competitiveness.

Distinct differences were identified also in the allocation methods used across enterprises of various sizes, particularly among manufacturing and service-oriented companies.

In manufacturing enterprises, smaller firms tend to rely predominantly on the surcharge (overhead rate) method, while larger manufacturing firms more frequently apply the division method using ratio numbers. This shift suggests a gradual transition toward more structured and proportional cost allocation systems as the scale and complexity of operations increase.

In contrast, service enterprises show an inverse trend—smaller service providers often use the surcharge method as well, due to its simplicity and lower administrative demands.

When disregarding both enterprise type and size, the overall analysis indicates that the most commonly used method for allocating indirect costs is the division method using ratio numbers (29.85%), followed by the simple division method (28.36%), the surcharge method (23.88%), and finally the ABC method (17.91%), which remains the least utilized.

From the perspective of controlling and cost management, these results reveal important patterns in how companies approach the precision and sophistication of indirect cost allocation.

In a broader managerial context, the choice of cost allocation method reflects the maturity of the company's controlling system. While traditional and simpler methods may suffice for operational cost tracking, the transition to ratio-based or activity-based approaches represents a strategic step toward integrated performance management and value-oriented control.

Ultimately, the results underscore that developing an appropriate allocation methodology is a crucial determinant of controlling effectiveness, cost accuracy, and managerial agility in today's competitive environment.

Use of Performance-Based Depreciation in Controlling

There are numerous methods of calculating depreciation. Within financial accounting, the obligation to determine the depreciation of fixed assets as accurately as possible arises from accounting legislation, ensuring that the depreciation value faithfully represents the actual wear and tear of the asset.

In controlling, however, depreciation can also be expressed in performance-based terms, for example, per unit of production, per machine hour, or per operating cycle.

The survey results indicate that the majority of companies use the same depreciation methods in controlling as in financial accounting, most commonly the straight-line method. This preference is mainly due to its computational simplicity and ease of integration with financial reporting systems. Only about 32% of enterprises apply performance-based depreciation methods within their controlling systems.

Performance-based depreciation is used most frequently by manufacturing companies, followed by service enterprises. This pattern can be explained by the fact that these types of companies have a higher proportion of fixed assets, particularly in the form of machinery, equipment, instruments, and buildings (such as production halls).

Although performance-based depreciation is more demanding in terms of calculation and reporting, it provides substantially higher explanatory and analytical value compared to traditional methods. It allows depreciation expenses to be directly linked to the actual utilization of assets, thus offering a more realistic representation of cost behavior in relation to production output or operational activity.

From a controlling perspective, the method of depreciation has a significant influence on the accuracy of cost allocation, product costing, and performance evaluation. The widespread use of straight-line depreciation reflects the tendency of many companies to prioritize simplicity and compliance over analytical precision. While this approach ensures consistency with financial accounting, it may obscure the true relationship between asset usage and cost generation, especially in production-intensive environments.

In contrast, performance-based depreciation provides a more dynamic and informative tool for management decision-making. By linking depreciation directly to production volume, operating hours, or other activity measures, it enables controllers and managers to:

- Better understand marginal costs and capacity utilization,
- Identify periods of under- or overuse of production assets,
- Improve budget accuracy and forecasting of maintenance or replacement costs,
- Support activity-based costing (ABC) and process-oriented control models.

For manufacturing and service enterprises, which rely heavily on equipment and long-term tangible assets, performance-based depreciation enhances cost traceability and profitability analysis. It also allows for more accurate internal pricing and investment decision-making, since depreciation costs are proportionate to actual asset use rather than merely to the passage of time.

However, implementing performance-based depreciation requires robust data systems capable of tracking production metrics and integrating them with accounting records. Thus, its adoption reflects a higher level of maturity in the company's controlling system.

From a management standpoint, companies that adopt this method gain more actionable cost information, enabling strategic asset management, capacity planning, and optimization of resource utilization. In a broader sense, the use of performance-based depreciation bridges the gap between operational efficiency and financial accuracy, reinforcing the role of controlling as a tool for strategic management and performance steering.

Types of Analyzed Variances

The identification and analysis of variances represent the culminating activity within operational controlling. Once variances are detected, they must be evaluated and followed by corrective actions to ensure that managerial feedback loops are effective.

In practice, variances are usually determined on both the input and output sides. Within each of these categories, variances can be further classified as quantitative, qualitative, or as structural variances arising from changes in the composition of inputs or outputs (see theoretical framework).

In this research, the following types of variances and their combinations were analyzed:

- Variances in the quantity of material and labor consumed,
- Variances in variable manufacturing overhead,
- Variances in fixed costs,
- Variances from planned input prices,
- Variances from planned output (performance) prices,
- Variances arising from structural changes,
- Variances from planned costs and revenues,
- Variances from planned profit, and
- Variances compared to the previous period.

The analysis revealed that the most frequently occurring variances across enterprises are:

- Material and labor consumption variances,
- Variable manufacturing overhead variances, and
- Fixed cost variances.

When examining variances by company size, distinct patterns emerged:

- Micro-enterprises (0–9 employees) most often analyze variances in variable costs, fixed costs, and price variances.
- Small enterprises (10–49 employees) focus mainly on variances in variable costs.
- Medium-small enterprises (50–99 employees) show similar tendencies as micro-enterprises but place greater emphasis on the detailed analysis of fixed costs and qualitative variances related to both inputs and outputs.
- Medium-sized enterprises (100–499 employees) display a more complex approach: in addition to the aforementioned variance types, they also incorporate structural variances; analyzing changes in the composition of both inputs and, in some cases, outputs.

Overall, the findings show that companies rarely limit themselves to analyzing only one or two types of variances. Instead, most enterprises employ combinations of several variance types, reflecting the increasing complexity of their cost control and performance measurement systems.

From the standpoint of controlling, the systematic identification, analysis, and interpretation of variances are fundamental for maintaining effective feedback and performance control within an organization. The range and sophistication of variances analyzed reflect the maturity of the company's controlling system and its ability to transform financial data into managerially relevant information.

Enterprises that focus only on basic variances tend to manage primarily at the operational cost level, reacting to short-term inefficiencies. In contrast, firms that extend their variance analysis to include price, structural, and profit variances demonstrate a more strategic and integrated controlling approach, capable of linking operational deviations to overall financial performance.

For management, variance analysis serves as an early-warning system that identifies not only deviations from plans but also their root causes. For instance:

- Material and labor variances reveal issues in production efficiency or procurement,
- Overhead variances indicate problems in cost center management or capacity utilization, and
- Price and structural variances highlight external market dynamics or internal shifts in the product mix.

Such insights enable managers to adopt targeted corrective measures, refine budget assumptions, and enhance decision quality.

Moreover, enterprises that analyze qualitative and structural variances tend to have a more advanced performance management culture, as they go beyond quantitative measures and evaluate the value-adding effectiveness of activities. This holistic view supports continuous improvement, process optimization, and strategic adaptability.

In sum, the findings underline that the breadth of variance analysis is a reliable indicator of controlling sophistication. Companies employing multi-dimensional variance analysis, combining quantitative, qualitative, and structural elements, gain a more comprehensive understanding of performance drivers, achieve higher decision accuracy, and strengthen the overall management control system.

Internal Corporate Statements and Their Role in Controlling

Among the most commonly prepared internal corporate reports are the budgeted balance sheet, the budgeted income statement, and the cash flow budget. These internal reports can be prepared either for individual departments, divisions, or plants, or for the company as a whole.

However, a budget loses its meaning and effectiveness if it is prepared merely as a "breakdown" of top-level financial indicators into lower organizational levels without corresponding analytical justification or managerial responsibility. Such a top-down approach often results in formal and ineffective budgeting, disconnected from operational reality.

According to the survey results, almost 45% of companies do not prepare any internal reports at all. A closer look reveals that more than half of the companies with 0–99 employees do not compile such statements, whereas among companies with 100–249 employees, only about one quarter fail to prepare them.

The most significant component of internal reporting is the budget of profit and loss from the company's core operating activities, the foundation of which is the budgeted income statement. This statement typically includes three types of cost budgets:

- The budget of prime (unit) costs,
- The budget of direct costs for a specific product or service, and
- The budget of overhead costs.

Nearly one-third of all surveyed companies prepare a budgeted income statement, with a clear trend: the larger the company, the higher the likelihood that such a report is prepared.

The budgeted balance sheet and budgeted income statement are both prepared by approximately 17% of companies. The construction of the budgeted balance sheet requires a separation of assets, liabilities, and equity related to operating, investing, and financing activities, as well as a distinction between funding sources that incur capital costs (interest and dividends) and those that do not. Interestingly, both reports are most frequently compiled by companies with up to 9 employees and by larger enterprises (250–499 employees).

Only about 4% of companies prepare a cash flow budget. This report serves as a tool for managing solvency and liquidity, and it provides the basis for coordinating relationships between activities that generate and consume financial resources. The foundation of this approach lies in the budget of permanent financing needs, which quantifies the level of working capital, and in the budget of cash flows from core operations.

Importantly, only about 3% of all companies prepare all three key internal reports (the budgeted income statement, the budgeted balance sheet, and the cash flow budget) which indicates a relatively low level of comprehensive internal financial planning.

From a controlling perspective, internal reporting plays a crucial role in linking strategic objectives with operational performance. The absence or limited use of budgeted statements in many enterprises suggests insufficient development of internal planning and control systems, particularly in small and medium-sized enterprises (SMEs).

Companies that do not prepare internal reports often rely solely on financial accounting outputs, which provide only an ex post view of performance. In contrast, budgeted financial statements form the foundation for proactive controlling, enabling managers to forecast, plan, and control future performance.

The budgeted income statement is essential for managing profitability and cost efficiency, allowing for variance analysis between planned and actual results. The budgeted balance sheet provides insight into financial structure, asset utilization, and capital efficiency, while the cash flow budget is indispensable for maintaining liquidity, solvency, and investment capacity.

Enterprises that integrate all three statements within their controlling system gain a comprehensive framework for financial coordination, where the relationships between profit, capital, and cash flow are clearly quantified and controlled. Such integration enables:

- Improved financial stability forecasting,
- Enhanced decision support for investment and financing,
- More effective cost and working capital management, and
- Strengthened alignment between strategic goals and financial performance.

The observed trend, where larger companies are more likely to prepare detailed internal reports, reflects the increasing complexity of their operations and the corresponding need for structured financial control mechanisms. For smaller firms, adopting even simplified versions of these internal reports could significantly improve transparency, accountability, and decision quality.

From a management standpoint, the preparation and consistent use of internal budgets represent not only a technical exercise but a core element of managerial control culture. A well-designed internal reporting system transforms the budget from a static document into a dynamic management tool, enabling continuous monitoring, adaptive planning, and informed decision-making.

In conclusion, the findings emphasize that the preparation of internal financial statements is a key determinant of managerial effectiveness, financial foresight, and organizational resilience.

Table 4.12 provides additional information regarding the compilation of internal company reports by company size.

Critical Point Analysis

Critical point analysis (also referred to as break-even analysis) is a key analytical tool used within controlling to determine the target profit, manage fixed and variable costs, monitor pricing policies, plan production capacity, optimize the production program, compare investment decision alternatives, and define safety margins or security coefficients.

Table 4.12 Compilation of internal company reports according to company size

Compiling internal company statements	0–9 (%)	10–49 (%)	50–99 (%)	100–249 (%)	250–499 (%)
Budget income statement	0.00	23.81	40.00	52.63	33.33
Budget balance sheet and income statement	50.00	11.90	20.00	15.79	33.33
Cash flow budget	0.00	4.76	0.00	5.26	0.00
Budget balance sheet, budget income statement and cash flow budget	0.00	4.76	0.00	0.00	0.00
No internal company statements	50.00	54.76	40.00	26.32	33.33

Source Own processing

One of the best-known methods within this analytical framework is the determination of the break-even point, which identifies the level of sales or output at which total revenues equal total costs, resulting in neither profit nor loss.

The survey revealed that three-quarters of enterprises do not perform critical point analysis. When broken down by type of enterprise, the results are relatively balanced, showing no significant differences between manufacturing, service, or trading firms.

However, when analyzed by company size, notable patterns emerge. The analysis is least frequently conducted by companies with 10–49 employees, whereas it is most commonly prepared by enterprises with 10–49 and 100–249 employees. Among those that do perform critical point analysis, the majority are service companies, manufacturing firms, and hybrid enterprises that combine trading and service activities.

Overall, only about one-quarter of all surveyed companies apply this form of analysis in their controlling systems.

From a controlling perspective, the limited use of critical point analysis among enterprises represents a missed opportunity for proactive performance management. This method is a fundamental instrument of cost–volume–profit (CVP) analysis, enabling controllers and managers to understand the relationship between sales volume, cost structure, and profitability.

Regular application of critical point analysis allows companies to:

- Identify minimum sales volume required to avoid losses,
- Evaluate the impact of cost structure changes (e.g., increase in fixed costs or shift in variable costs),
- Support pricing and margin policy decisions,
- Determine optimal product mix in relation to contribution margins, and
- Assess the financial risk exposure through safety margins and operating leverage.

The absence of such analysis in many enterprises suggests a reactive rather than predictive approach to cost and profit management. Without critical point analysis, management lacks a quantitative basis for decision-making, relying instead on intuition or past performance, which can lead to inefficient pricing, suboptimal production planning, or investment errors.

For service and manufacturing companies, which typically have a significant share of fixed costs, critical point analysis provides valuable insight into capacity utilization, break-even turnover, and profit sensitivity to changes in demand or cost structure. It is especially relevant in volatile market conditions, where controlling systems must provide early warning indicators for shifts in financial equilibrium.

From a management standpoint, incorporating critical point analysis into regular controlling practice enhances the company's ability to:

- Translate financial data into operational performance targets,
- Simulate the financial effects of strategic decisions (e.g., price adjustments, product diversification, or investment expansion), and
- Strengthen strategic resilience through better understanding of risk thresholds.

In more mature controlling systems, break-even and sensitivity analyses are often integrated into scenario planning and budget simulations, providing management with quantified decision support for both short-term operations and long-term strategic planning.

In conclusion, the findings underscore that critical point analysis is not only a basic financial tool, but also a strategic instrument of controlling. Its wider adoption would substantially improve the analytical depth, foresight, and decision quality of management, contributing to more sustainable financial performance and better alignment between cost structures and strategic objectives.

4.4.2 Analysis of Strategic Controlling Tools

Strategic controlling focuses on maintaining existing and identifying and creating new success potentials. Its main task is to detect problems and deviations from the desired state before they become reflected in operational figures.

In practice, operational controlling tools are used more frequently than strategic ones; therefore, they were given greater attention in the previous part of the work.

Within the framework of strategic controlling tools, the following methods were examined:

- PEST analysis,
- Industry analysis,
- SWOT analysis,
- Portfolio analysis,
- Product life cycle analysis,
- KPI (Key Performance Indicators).

PEST Analysis

The purpose of the PEST analysis is to gather information about the external environment of the enterprise, to identify its changes and possible impacts on the company, and to determine the factors influencing the macro-environment and their effects on business operations. These factors typically include technological, political and legal, social, cultural, demographic, and economic influences.

According to the survey results, this method is not widely applied—82% of the surveyed companies do not conduct a PEST analysis. Among those that do, the method is used most frequently by enterprises with 10–49 employees and by larger companies with 250–499 employees. When viewed from the perspective of industry type, the analysis is conducted primarily by service-oriented enterprises, which account for 45% of all companies that apply this method.

From a controlling perspective, PEST analysis plays a crucial role in strategic planning and early warning systems. Although it is not an accounting or numerical tool in itself, it provides contextual input for strategic controlling, linking external macroeconomic and institutional developments to internal corporate performance indicators.

The low adoption rate of PEST analysis among companies suggests that many enterprises still perceive controlling primarily as an operational and cost-based function, rather than as a strategic management system. However, integrating PEST analysis into the controlling framework can significantly enhance long-term planning, risk assessment, and scenario management.

Specifically, incorporating PEST findings into strategic controlling enables companies to:

- Anticipate external threats and opportunities that may affect cost structures, demand, or financing conditions,
- Align budgetary and investment planning with expected macroeconomic trends,
- Identify regulatory and technological shifts that may require strategic adaptation, and
- Strengthen the link between environmental monitoring and financial strategy.

For controllers and management, PEST analysis serves as a decision-support tool for interpreting the broader business environment. It allows them to translate qualitative insights into quantitative forecasts and risk-adjusted budgets.

In mature controlling systems, PEST analysis becomes a component of integrated strategic dashboards, supporting Key Performance Indicators (KPIs) that reflect not only internal efficiency but also the company's ability to adapt to external changes.

In summary, while PEST analysis is underutilized, its systematic integration into controlling processes can transform the company's approach from reactive financial management to proactive strategic controlling, thereby improving resilience, adaptability, and long-term competitiveness.

Table 4.13 provides additional information.

Table 4.13 PEST analysis in companies divided by number of employees

PEST analysis	0–9 (%)	10–49 (%)	50–99 (%)	100–249 (%)	250–499 (%)	Total (%)
Yes	0.00	28.57	10.00	0.00	33.33	17.72
No	100.00	71.43	90.00	100.00	66.67	82.28

Source Own processing

Industry Analysis (Porter's Five Forces Model)

Industry analysis, also known as the Five Forces Model, is based on the premise that industries differ in their profit potential, and that the combined strength of five competitive forces determines the intensity of competition and, consequently, the profitability potential of the sector.

- As described in detail in the theoretical framework, these five forces include:
- Threat of substitutes,
- Bargaining power of suppliers,
- Bargaining power of customers,
- Threat of potential entrants, and
- Rivalry among existing competitors.

Unlike the PEST analysis, the industry analysis shows the opposite trend in terms of its use. It is applied by more than 67% of surveyed companies, making it one of the most commonly used strategic tools in controlling practice. The analysis is most frequently utilized by companies with 50–249 employees, while small enterprises with up to 10 employees use it the least. Interestingly, all companies with 50–99 employees reported using industry analysis.

A more detailed breakdown by industry type revealed that the method is applied primarily by service-oriented enterprises (16.46%) and manufacturing companies (20.25%).

From a controlling perspective, industry analysis provides an essential external analytical foundation for strategic planning, performance benchmarking, and risk management. It enables controllers and managers to identify the structural characteristics of the market, assess competitive pressures, and evaluate the sustainability of profit margins within their industry.

The relatively high adoption of this analysis indicates that many firms recognize the need to align internal performance metrics with external market dynamics. By integrating industry analysis into controlling, companies can:

- Link strategic objectives and financial targets to the competitive conditions of their market,
- Assess how changes in supplier or customer power affect cost structures and profitability,
- Anticipate market entry threats or substitute innovations that could erode market share, and

Table 4.14 Conducting industry analysis in enterprises classified by number of employees

Industry analysis	0–9 (%)	10–49 (%)	50–99 (%)	100–249 (%)	250–499 (%)	Total (%)
Yes	25.00	61.90	100.00	75.00	33.33	67.09
No	75.00	38.10	0.00	25.00	66.67	32.91

Source:own processing

- Support investment and capacity planning through a clearer understanding of industry cycles and competition intensity.

For controllers, the Five Forces Model provides a structured framework for strategic variance analysis—explaining deviations in profitability or sales performance not by internal inefficiencies, but by external competitive pressures. Integrating this model with traditional controlling instruments (such as budgeting, KPI dashboards, or profitability analysis) enhances the strategic orientation of controlling and shifts its focus from cost monitoring to strategic performance management.

From a management standpoint, the use of industry analysis within controlling enables a forward-looking perspective:

- It facilitates scenario analysis and strategic simulations,
- Provides input for target costing and market-based pricing, and
- Helps to identify critical success factors that determine long-term competitiveness.

In more mature controlling systems, insights from industry analysis are embedded into balanced scorecards or strategic control panels, ensuring that key performance indicators (KPIs) reflect not only internal efficiency but also the company's position within its competitive environment.

In summary, industry analysis serves as a bridge between strategic management and controlling, translating external market forces into quantifiable performance indicators. Its integration into controlling practice strengthens the company's ability to anticipate change, adapt strategy, and maintain profitability in dynamic competitive conditions (Table 4.14).

SWOT Analysis

The SWOT analysis examines both the internal and external environments of an enterprise. The analysis of the internal environment identifies the company's strengths and weaknesses, while the analysis of the external environment reveals opportunities and threats. Based on various combinations of these four elements, strategies are formulated that the company should pursue in order to strengthen its market position, improve performance, or mitigate risks.

According to the survey results, approximately half of the companies conduct SWOT analysis and half do not (56%). As illustrated in the data, companies with up to 99 employees generally do not perform SWOT analysis, while those with 100 to

499 employees conduct it more frequently. From the perspective of industry type, the analysis is most commonly carried out by service-oriented and manufacturing companies (together accounting for 23.08% of all surveyed firms), mirroring the trend observed in the previous analyses.

From a controlling perspective, SWOT analysis represents a vital link between strategic assessment and performance management. Although it is primarily a qualitative tool, its results provide the contextual foundation for quantitative controlling instruments, such as budgeting, KPI systems, and variance analysis.

By integrating SWOT analysis into controlling practice, companies can:

- Align internal strengths (e.g., production efficiency, financial stability, skilled labor) with strategic opportunities in the market,
- Identify internal weaknesses that may lead to unfavorable financial deviations or inefficiencies,
- Quantify the potential impact of external threats (e.g., regulatory changes, technological shifts) on costs, revenues, or liquidity, and
- Support strategic scenario planning by connecting qualitative insights with measurable financial indicators.

For controllers, SWOT analysis serves as a diagnostic framework that enriches traditional reporting systems. When incorporated into the controlling cycle—planning, measurement, analysis, and correction—it allows for the creation of strategically oriented KPIs that go beyond short-term operational data. For example, identified weaknesses can be translated into cost-reduction objectives, while opportunities may be reflected in revenue-growth targets or investment priorities.

The lower utilization rate of SWOT analysis among smaller enterprises reflects the fact that many lack formalized strategic controlling processes. However, even simplified SWOT assessments can significantly improve strategic awareness, helping small and medium-sized enterprises (SMEs) establish structured feedback mechanisms between their external environment and internal operations.

From a management viewpoint, SWOT analysis enhances strategic decision-making by offering a clear overview of the organization's position within its environment. When systematically connected with controlling tools, it enables evidence-based strategy formulation, ensures coherence between strategic and operational goals, and strengthens the company's adaptive capacity.

In conclusion, SWOT analysis, when integrated into the controlling framework, transforms from a static descriptive method into a dynamic management instrument—providing the foundation for strategic control, proactive risk management, and sustainable performance improvement (Table 4.15).

Portfolio Analysis

The purpose of portfolio analysis is to concentrate company resources in areas where favorable market conditions are expected and where the enterprise can capitalize on its competitive advantages.

Table 4.15 Conducting SWOT analysis in enterprises classified by number of employees

SWOT analysis	0–9 (%)	10–49 (%)	50–99 (%)	100–249 (%)	250–499 (%)	Total (%)
Yes	25.00	40.48	30.00	57.89	66.67	43.59
No	75.00	59.52	70.00	42.11	33.33	56.41

Source Own processing

To conduct such an analysis, it is first necessary to define and group products or business units according to their technical functions, performance, and target customers. This segmentation enables the company to evaluate the relative attractiveness and competitive strength of each product group, forming the basis for strategic investment and divestment decisions.

Despite its strategic importance, the survey shows that less than 28% of companies perform portfolio analysis. As indicated in the following data, the analysis is most frequently carried out by companies with 50–249 employees (a total of 77.27% within this size group). From the perspective of industry type, the analysis is most common among manufacturing and service companies, together representing 50% of all enterprises that use this method.

Notably, among micro-enterprises (0–9 employees), portfolio analysis is conducted only by trading companies that also provide services. Conversely, among larger enterprises with 250–499 employees, the analysis is performed exclusively by service-oriented firms.

From a controlling perspective, portfolio analysis is a powerful strategic management and resource allocation tool. It provides controllers and managers with a structured framework for evaluating the profitability, growth potential, and risk exposure of individual business units, product lines, or market segments.

In controlling practice, portfolio analysis enables companies to:

- Link financial performance indicators with market and competitive parameters,
- Identify cash-generating units that can finance innovation or expansion,
- Detect underperforming or low-potential products that should be restructured or discontinued, and
- Support strategic budgeting by prioritizing investments in high-potential segments.

The limited application of portfolio analysis suggests that many firms focus mainly on short-term operational control rather than strategic portfolio management. Yet, for medium-sized and large enterprises, integrating portfolio analysis into controlling provides a comprehensive basis for capital allocation, profitability optimization, and long-term sustainability.

For controllers, this method is especially valuable in connecting non-financial factors (such as market position, product life cycle stage, or technological competence) with financial outcomes like cash flow, ROI, or contribution margin. When embedded in the controlling system, portfolio analysis becomes a quantitative complement to strategic tools such as SWOT and industry analysis, allowing for more evidence-based strategic decision-making.

From a management standpoint, portfolio analysis enhances the company's ability to maintain strategic balance between profitable core products and emerging growth opportunities. It supports resource optimization, ensuring that investments are directed toward products or business units with the highest long-term return potential.

In advanced controlling systems, portfolio analysis is frequently integrated with Balanced Scorecard frameworks and KPI dashboards, where each strategic business unit is monitored not only for financial results but also for its strategic contribution to the company's overall success.

In conclusion, portfolio analysis represents an essential bridge between strategic planning and controlling. Its systematic use allows companies to transform strategic insights into quantified investment priorities, improving decision transparency, resource efficiency, and long-term competitiveness.

Product Life Cycle Analysis

The concept of product life cycle (PLC) analysis is based on the fact that every product, during its time on the market, passes through four distinct phases—introduction, growth, maturity, and decline—as outlined in the theoretical section of this work.

In each of these stages, companies must account for changes in revenues and cash flow, as both fluctuate depending on product performance, market conditions, and competitive dynamics. The method provides businesses with an understanding of whether their production and sales program is balanced, and whether they are effectively managing products at different stages of maturity.

According to the conducted research, this method is used very rarely, applied by less than 12% of the surveyed enterprises. It is utilized primarily by medium-sized companies with 10–49 employees, which represent 55.56% of all firms that use the method. In contrast, micro-enterprises (up to 9 employees) apply it in only 11.11% of cases among those using the method. From the perspective of industry type, manufacturing companies make the most use of the analysis (over 33%), followed by service-oriented companies (over 22%).

From a controlling perspective, product life cycle (PLC) analysis is an essential strategic management and performance monitoring tool that enables enterprises to link product strategy with financial planning and control. By mapping products across their life cycle stages, controllers can better anticipate changes in revenues, costs, profitability, and cash flow, thus ensuring a balanced and sustainable product portfolio.

The low utilization rate of PLC analysis among companies indicates that many organizations still lack strategic controlling frameworks capable of connecting product development and market dynamics with financial performance management.

However, the integration of this method into controlling offers several significant benefits:

- It allows for early identification of declining products that require innovation, repositioning, or withdrawal.
- It supports strategic investment decisions by highlighting which products are in growth and should receive further financial support.
- It improves profitability forecasting by linking product maturity to expected cost and revenue patterns.
- It enables the creation of dynamic budgeting models, where financial plans reflect the actual life cycle stage of each product.

For controllers, PLC analysis serves as a valuable complement to traditional financial controlling tools. It allows the transformation of qualitative product insights into quantifiable performance metrics such as contribution margin, ROI, or payback period. When used in conjunction with portfolio analysis and KPI systems, PLC analysis strengthens the company's ability to evaluate product performance not only in absolute financial terms but also in strategic relevance.

From a management perspective, PLC analysis enhances decision-making by providing visibility into the timing and balance of innovation, marketing, and production efforts. It helps ensure that the company maintains an optimal mix of growth, mature, and declining products, thus reducing dependency on a single revenue stream and promoting long-term stability.

In more advanced controlling systems, the outcomes of PLC analysis are incorporated into strategic dashboards and Balanced Scorecards, allowing real-time monitoring of product profitability, market share development, and innovation success rates.

In conclusion, the integration of product life cycle analysis into controlling enables companies to transform their understanding of product performance from a purely marketing perspective into a comprehensive financial and strategic management tool. Although its current use is limited, wider adoption would significantly enhance strategic planning, cost management, and investment effectiveness, contributing to sustainable competitiveness and balanced portfolio management.

KPI (Key Performance Indicators)

The primary purpose of Key Performance Indicators (KPIs) is to provide the most realistic and measurable assessment of the success or failure of a specific activity, process, or area within an organization. Success can refer to achieving long-term strategic goals as well as regular fulfillment of operational targets within individual processes.

According to the survey, more than half of the analyzed enterprises (almost 60%) evaluate KPIs as part of their performance management system. The evaluation of performance indicators is most common among medium-sized companies with 10–249 employees, representing 91.30% of all enterprises that use KPIs. When analyzed by industry type, manufacturing companies (39.13%) and service providers (26.09%) are the main users of performance indicators. Further detailed results are presented in the following table.

From a controlling perspective, the use of KPIs is one of the core elements of modern performance management. KPIs translate strategic objectives into quantifiable metrics, enabling continuous monitoring, evaluation, and control of company performance across all levels of management.

For controllers, KPIs serve as a bridge between strategy and operations. They allow the integration of financial indicators (e.g., revenue growth, ROI, cost efficiency) with non-financial measures (e.g., customer satisfaction, process quality, innovation rate), thereby creating a comprehensive view of organizational performance.

The widespread use of KPIs among medium-sized companies demonstrates that these firms already recognize the importance of measurable management systems and the need to transform strategic goals into operationally relevant data. However, in many organizations, KPI systems are still underdeveloped—focusing mainly on financial indicators rather than including strategic, process, and value-based metrics.

Integrating KPIs into the controlling framework offers several key advantages:

- Enables target-oriented management by linking budgets and strategic plans with measurable outcomes,
- Facilitates variance analysis by providing benchmarks against planned results,
- Supports early warning systems that identify performance deviations and risks,
- Enhances cross-departmental coordination by establishing shared goals and accountability, and
- Promotes strategic alignment by cascading objectives from corporate level to operational units.

For management, KPI-based controlling provides decision-relevant insights for both short-term corrective actions and long-term strategic adjustments. By focusing on the most critical success factors, managers can prioritize initiatives, allocate resources effectively, and ensure continuous performance improvement.

In advanced controlling systems, KPIs are integrated into Balanced Scorecards, management dashboards, and performance reporting tools, allowing real-time monitoring of key results and the visualization of trends. Such integration enhances the organization's ability to manage by objectives, strengthens data-driven decision-making, and embeds strategic control within daily operations.

In conclusion, Key Performance Indicators represent one of the most powerful tools in the controlling arsenal. When properly defined, measured, and analyzed, KPIs transform abstract strategic goals into actionable control information, enabling enterprises to improve performance transparency, accountability, and strategic coherence. The effective use of KPIs thus signifies a mature controlling culture, where decision-making is grounded in evidence, foresight, and continuous improvement (Table 4.16).

Table 4.16 Evaluation of KPIs in enterprises classified by number of employees

KPI	0–9 (%)	10–49 (%)	50–99 (%)	100–249 (%)	250–499 (%)	Total (%)
Yes	4.35	47.83	15.22	28.26	4.35	100.00
No	6.45	64.52	6.45	19.35	3.23	100.00

Source Own processing

Chapter 5
Discussion

According to Eschenbach and Siller (2012), the most important goal of controlling is to support top management in effective corporate governance. Its partial objectives include ensuring both anticipation and adaptability—meaning that controlling records and analyzes information about past, current, and expected future changes in the internal and external environment of the enterprise. On the basis of such information, controlling enables management to react proactively to future developments.

This clearly demonstrates that controlling is an integral component of corporate management, serving as both a decision-support and coordination system. In this research, controlling was analyzed both in relation to financial indicators derived from balance sheets and income statements of individual enterprises, and in terms of the extent to which controlling tools are utilized by companies.

In general, controlling is recommended primarily for small, medium, and large enterprises. Micro-enterprises typically do not have a formalized controlling system but instead apply selected methods and tools that serve their immediate needs. This finding was confirmed by the survey results: enterprises with more than 100 employees tend to use controlling more frequently.

Smaller enterprises, by contrast, rely mostly on operational controlling tools such as cost calculations, budgeting, and variance analysis. Similar patterns were observed among enterprises with foreign ownership, which tend to be larger and almost always have controlling implemented, either internally or through their parent company's controlling department.

From the perspective of company turnover, controlling is most often implemented by companies with annual revenues exceeding CZK 100 million. The main reasons cited by companies that do not have controlling in place include insufficient financial resources, the perceived lack of necessity, reliance on financial accounting data for decision-making, or the small size of the company, which they believe does not justify a comprehensive management control system.

M. Vlčková, *Controlling as a Business Process Management Tool*, Contributions to Finance and Accounting, https://doi.org/10.1007/978-3-032-27526-4_5

Controlling is most widely used in manufacturing enterprises (64%). This is because manufacturing processes are generally more complex than those in trading firms, which mostly engage in buying and selling. Manufacturing companies thus have a greater need for detailed analysis, cost calculation, cost classification, and product portfolio planning. Controlling is also commonly applied in service enterprises, which typically focus on operational tools such as cost, efficiency, and performance analysis, as well as costing systems.

Financial Structure and Controlling Implications

A statistical analysis of balance sheet indicators confirmed that enterprises with implemented controlling tend to have higher levels of both receivables and liabilities, particularly short-term liabilities. This positive correlation suggests active management of both payables and receivables; however, a mismatch (i.e., lower receivables and higher liabilities) could negatively affect liquidity and indebtedness indicators.

It was further found that companies with controlling exhibit a higher share of external financing sources, likely due to greater investment in fixed assets. Although the difference in fixed asset value was not statistically significant, it was nonetheless higher in companies using controlling. Similarly, share capital values are higher in such enterprises, reflecting their larger size and stronger capitalization.

From the perspective of income statement analysis, companies with controlling show higher revenues from the sale of own products and services, as well as higher personnel costs. These findings confirm that controlling is predominantly implemented in larger enterprises with higher turnover and more employees, where both sales and wage costs are proportionally higher.

Interestingly, the corporate income tax indicator is higher in companies without controlling, which may be due to the fact that controlled companies report higher costs, both in terms of personnel expenses and depreciation of tangible and intangible assets, resulting in lower taxable income.

Companies with controlling also show lower net financial results, which may be explained by higher interest expenses due to greater indebtedness. Indicators such as total indebtedness, debt-to-equity ratio, and interest burden are all higher among companies that have controlling implemented. Conversely, firms without controlling show higher equity ratios, reflecting their lower reliance on external debt financing.

Profitability indicators such as return on assets (ROA), return on sales (ROS), and return on costs (ROC) are higher in enterprises without controlling, primarily because these firms have higher accounting profit relative to smaller asset and cost bases.

Liquidity indicators also tend to favor companies without controlling, likely due to their lower liabilities and higher proportion of liquid assets relative to total assets.

However, the results of bankruptcy and creditworthiness models (e.g., Taffler's model, Quick Test, and IN99 model) reveal that companies without controlling achieve slightly better results. This could be attributed to higher indebtedness and greater use of foreign capital among controlled companies, which, while riskier, often accompanies higher investment and growth orientation.

Operational and Strategic Controlling Tools

A substantial part of the study analyzed the use of operational and strategic controlling tools. Controlling methods and instruments should be applied only when preliminary analysis indicates that their use will yield tangible benefits, either at the level of individual departments or for the enterprise as a whole. Employing all tools indiscriminately can sometimes be counterproductive, due to time and cost demands.

Operational Controlling

The analysis of operational controlling covered the following areas:

- Integration of controlling within the organizational structure: Internal controlling is more common than external controlling, with external services used by only 14% of enterprises, mostly smaller ones. Internal controlling departments are usually placed at staff level, focusing on decision preparation, coordination of sub-plans, and control, rather than on direct decision-making.
- Managerial accounting systems: Two-circle accounting systems (separating financial and managerial accounting) are typically used by larger enterprises, especially manufacturing ones, whereas single-circle systems prevail among smaller firms.
- Operational planning: The frequency of plan preparation depends more on business type and process structure than on company size.
- Cost classification: The variable/fixed cost structure is more data-intensive and thus used mainly by larger companies, while smaller firms continue to classify costs traditionally into direct and indirect or prime and overhead.
- Costing formulas and methods: The traditional costing formula, based on direct and indirect costs, remains the most widely used, despite being considered outdated in theory. The retrograde formula (based on variable and fixed costs) and the Activity-Based Costing (ABC) method are used less frequently; the latter by only 18% of companies, mainly due to its data complexity.
- Indirect cost allocation methods: The division with ratio numbers method is the most common, followed by simple division and the surcharge method. Their popularity stems from their simplicity and low data requirements.
- Performance-based depreciation: Used by about one-third of enterprises, mainly manufacturing and service firms, as it provides higher informational value but is computationally more demanding.
- Variance analysis: Most firms employ combinations of variance types (cost, quantity, price, structure), particularly those with heterogeneous production. Timely variance evaluation allows rapid corrective action.
- Internal reporting: Preparing internal reports is a resource-intensive process, typically performed by larger firms with developed controlling systems. Smaller firms often prepare only basic cost, revenue, and financing plans.

Strategic Controlling

The study also analyzed the use of strategic tools, including PEST analysis, industry analysis, SWOT analysis, portfolio analysis, product life cycle analysis, and Key

Performance Indicators (KPIs). Strategic tools are used much less frequently than operational ones due to data collection complexity and the rapid obsolescence of results in today's turbulent environment.

The most notable development in recent years has been the widespread adoption of KPI systems, which provide customized performance metrics tailored to specific activities, processes, departments, or entire companies—in both financial and non-financial terms.

Broader Implications for Controlling Practice

The overall analysis confirms that controlling is a key driver of managerial effectiveness and a fundamental pillar of data-based decision-making. However, its implementation and depth of application vary widely by company size, sector, and ownership structure.

For smaller enterprises, the priority should be to introduce simplified forms of controlling, focusing on essential tools such as budgeting, cost tracking, and variance analysis. For larger firms, the challenge lies in integrating operational and strategic controlling, ensuring that financial data, performance indicators, and strategic objectives form a coherent management control system.

Ultimately, controlling transforms information into insight, bridging financial accounting and strategic management, and provides companies with the analytical capability to anticipate, adapt, and sustain competitive success in an increasingly dynamic business environment.

Based on the above analyses, several weak points in the use of controlling tools were identified, and corresponding recommendations for their optimization were formulated, including guidelines for enterprises.

For the sake of simplicity and clarity, enterprises were divided into two main categories: small and large companies (individual tools were analyzed in greater detail in previous sections).

Small enterprises are defined as those with up to 50 employees and annual turnover below CZK 100 million, large enterprises exceed these thresholds.

The following section specifies operational controlling tools that may represent potential weaknesses, as strategic controlling tools tend to be used primarily by larger enterprises.

For small companies, it is recommended to adopt methods such as industry analysis or Key Performance Indicator (KPI) evaluation, which can significantly enhance the quality of management decision-making.

The recommendations summarized in Table 5.1 are intended to help eliminate weaknesses in the implementation and optimization of controlling systems, and to support enterprises in building a more effective, data-driven management structure.

Implications for Controlling

From a controlling and management perspective, these recommendations underscore the importance of scaling controlling tools according to company size, complexity, and resource availability.

Table 5.1 Recommended tools for optimizing operational controlling in small and large enterprises

Operational controlling tools	Small enterprises	Large enterprises
Integration of controlling into the organizational structure	External controlling	Internal controlling as a staff or line department
Managerial accounting system	Single-circle accounting system	Dual-circle accounting system or a combination of both
Preparation of operational plans	3 months–1 year	As needed
Cost classification (prime/overhead, direct/indirect, variable/fixed)	Classification into prime and overhead or direct and indirect costs	Classification into variable and fixed costs combined with direct and indirect costs
Types of costing formulas and methods used	Traditional costing formula; cost and price calculation	Retrograde costing formula; preliminary, price, and final cost calculations
Methods for allocating indirect costs	Surcharge method; simple division method	Division with ratio numbers; Activity-Based Costing (ABC) method
Use of performance-based depreciation	Linear depreciation	Performance-based depreciation
Types of variances analyzed	Quantitative and qualitative input (and possibly output) variances	Quantitative and qualitative variances of both inputs and outputs, including structural variances
Frequency of variance evaluation	Final—after completion of production, activity, or process	Preliminary, ongoing, and final evaluation at shorter time intervals
Preparation of internal reports	Budgeted income statement or cash flow budget	Budgeted balance sheet, income statement, and cash flow budget

Source Own processing

For small enterprises, the primary goal should be to establish a simplified but functional controlling framework, focusing on basic planning, cost control, and performance evaluation. Tools such as traditional costing, simple variance analysis, and cash flow budgeting can significantly improve financial transparency and decision-making efficiency, even with limited data and personnel.

For larger enterprises, the challenge lies in achieving integration and sophistication. The use of dual accounting systems, retrograde costing, activity-based costing (ABC), and multi-level internal reporting enables comprehensive cost transparency, performance accountability, and strategic coordination across departments.

Implementing performance-based depreciation, complex variance analysis, and structured reporting systems allows large firms to move from reactive cost management to proactive performance steering, the core mission of controlling.

In both cases, the optimization of operational controlling tools must be accompanied by the gradual introduction of strategic controlling methods such as KPI monitoring, industry and portfolio analyses, and life cycle management. Integrating these tools ensures that operational efficiency aligns with strategic objectives, ultimately strengthening the company's resilience, competitiveness, and long-term profitability.

Chapter 6
Conclusion

The primary purpose of controlling is to coordinate management systems so that information needs are covered and internal as well as external harmonization is ensured. According to Reichmann (1997), the controlling system consists of several components that must be organizationally defined and then analyzed and structured, both through operational tools and long-term, strategic instruments. These components include goals (for the company as a whole and for individual organizational units), tasks, concepts, and applications.

The objective of this monograph was to position controlling within the management process and to analyze the use of operational and strategic controlling tools and their linkage to the overall management system. The partial objectives were (i) to analyze controlling in the Czech Republic in relation to financial indicators, (ii) to identify weak points, and (iii) to propose solutions to optimize the controlling process. Both operational and strategic tools were evaluated, and enterprises with and without controlling were analyzed.

Theoretical Framework

The first part defined controlling, its importance, objectives, and functions, and described the role of the controller within the company and across internal units. A brief overview of the evolution of controlling was included to clarify how linkages and processes have developed over time. A substantial section presented controlling instruments that allow both performance measurement and forecasting in the short, medium, and long term, and explained their impact on business processes. The operational and strategic tools covered represent those most commonly used in practice, forming the basis for the empirical results that constitute the core of this monograph.

Empirical Basis and Methods

The empirical analysis combined quantitative and qualitative data—survey responses from 245 enterprises and financial data for 160 enterprises retrieved from the Albertina Gold Edition database. Methods included observation, questionnaire

M. Vlčková, *Controlling as a Business Process Management Tool*, Contributions to Finance and Accounting, https://doi.org/10.1007/978-3-032-27526-4_6

inquiry, analysis, synthesis, logical induction and deduction, description, and comparison. For statistical testing, the non-parametric Mann–Whitney U test was applied.

Results—Part I: General Characteristics of Firms With/Without Controlling

The first part compared firms with and without controlling by basic characteristics (size, geography, type, etc.). The share of firms with controlling increases with employee headcount. By type, controlling is used primarily in manufacturing and service firms. Although differences by turnover were not statistically significant, graphical inspection suggests controlling is more prevalent among firms with turnover above CZK 100 million. As expected, firms with foreign participation mostly have controlling in place.

Results—Part II: Financial Structure and Performance Indicators

Using statistical tests, we assessed selected assets and liabilities, costs, revenues, and earnings, and a set of financial ratios (indebtedness, liquidity, profitability, bankruptcy/creditworthiness models) in relation to the presence of controlling.

- Firms with controlling show higher trade receivables and total receivables (assets) and higher share capital, total liabilities, external capital, and short-term liabilities (liabilities).
- They also report higher sales of own products and services and higher personnel costs. In contrast, income tax on ordinary activities is higher in firms without controlling.
- Financial result from financial activities tends to be lower in firms with controlling—consistent with higher interest expense from a greater debt share.
- Indebtedness indicators (total indebtedness, debt-to-equity, interest burden) are significantly higher in firms with controlling; conversely, the equity ratio is higher in firms without controlling.
- Liquidity indicators are generally better for firms without controlling.
- Profitability (ROA, ROS, ROC) is higher among firms without controlling, driven by higher accounting profit relative to their smaller asset, sales, and cost bases.
- Bankruptcy/creditworthiness models (Taffler, IN99, Quick Test) also yield more favorable values for firms without controlling—likely reflecting lower leverage and lower risk profiles.

Controlling implication: These results do not imply that controlling harms performance. Rather, firms that adopt controlling tend to be larger, more leveraged, and more investment-intensive, which temporarily depresses profitability and liquidity but often supports growth, capacity expansion, and information quality. Interpreting ratios must therefore be context-sensitive: maturity, leverage policy, sector specifics, and growth phase materially affect outcomes.

Results—Part III: Use of Operational and Strategic Tools

Enterprises were then analyzed by size (employees) and type. The most common arrangement is internal controlling at the staff level. Managerial accounting is more often run in a single-circle system (analytical records), especially among smaller firms. Operational plans are typically annual.

A major section addressed cost classification and costing. Most firms classify costs as variable vs. fixed; price calculations dominate; indirect costs are allocated mainly by the division with ratio numbers method. The most frequent variances are material and labor usage, variable manufacturing overhead, and fixed cost variances. Few firms compile critical point (break-even) analyses or internal budget statements. In strategic controlling, industry analysis and KPIs are used most; fewer than half apply PEST, SWOT, portfolio, or product life-cycle analyses.

Controlling implication: Tool choice mirrors resource intensity. Operational tools prevail where quick, decision-relevant information is required. Strategic tools are underused due to data demands and rapid obsolescence, a gap that advanced controlling can close through streamlined data pipelines and scenario dashboards.

Recommendations and Optimization

The concluding part formulates recommendations to optimize the use of controlling tools in Czech enterprises, detailing operational instruments that often become bottlenecks and proposing practical remedies (e.g., fit-for-purpose planning horizons, cost classification aligned with costing formulas, proportionate variance analysis, progressive adoption of ABC where feasible).

Theoretical and Practical Contribution

This book offers a comprehensive perspective on controlling with emphasis on methods and tools. It verifies links between selected financial indicators and controlling, analyzes controlling practices in enterprises, and provides recommendations for embedding controlling into business practice.

Managerial Takeaway

Effective controlling is not "more tools at any cost," but the right mix, scaled to firm size, complexity, and strategy—integrating operational reliability (budgeting, costing, variances) with strategic foresight (industry forces, KPIs, portfolio/PLC), and translating both into coherent, decision-ready information for management.

References

Ahmad, T., & Van Looy, A. (2020). Business process management and digital innovations: A systematic literature review. *Sustainability, 12*(17), 6827. https://doi.org/10.3390/su12176827

Budíková, M., Králová, M., & Maroš, B. (2010). *Průvodce základními statistickými metodami.* 1. vyd. Grada Publishing.

Bui, N. T., Tu Le, O. T., & Nguyen, P. T. T. (2020). Management accounting practices among Vietnamese small and medium enterprises. *Asian Economic and Financial Review, 10*(1), 94–115. https://doi.org/10.18488/journal.aefr.2020.101.94.115

Cornel, G., & Lavinia-Maria, G. (2012). Controlling - A useful tool for top management. *Analele Universitatii Maritime Constanta, 13*(18), 305–308.

Čebukina, M. V., et al. (2013). Controlling as a tool for implementation of the system for the enterprise resource potential management in its capitalized form. *World Applied Sciences Journal, 27*(4), 444–447.

Čechová, A. (2011). *Manažerské účetnictví*. Brno: Computer Press.

Czech Republic. (2002). *České účetní standardy pro účetní jednotky, které účtují podle vyhlášky č. 500/2002 Sb., ve znění pozdějších předpisů.*

Drury, C. (2023). *Management and cost accounting.* 12th Reed. Cengage Learning.

Eschenbach, R. (2004). *Controlling.* 2. vyd. ASPI.

Eschenbach, R., & Siller, H. (2012). *Profesionální controlling. Koncepce a nástroje.* Wolters Kluwer.

Fibírová, J. (2003). *Reporting.* 2. vyd. Grada Publishing.

Fibírová, J., Šoljaková, L., Wagner, J., & Petera, P. (2020). *Manažerské účetnictví: nástroje a metody* (3. upravené vydání). Wolters Kluwer.

Fotr, J. (2012). *Tvorba strategie a strategické plánování: teorie a praxe.* Grada Publishing.

Fotr, J., Dědina, J., & Hrůzová, H. (2003). *Manažerské rozhodování*. 3. vyd. Ekopress.

Freund, R. J., Wilson, W. J., & Mohr, D. L. (2010). *Statistical methods* (3rd ed.). Elsevier.

Horváth & Partners. (2004). *Nová koncepce controllingu: Cesta k účinnému controllingu.* Profess consulting.

Horváth, & Partners. (2019). *The controlling concept: Cornerstone of performance management.* Verlag Franz Vahlen.

Horváth, P. (2002). *Controlling.* Verlag Franz Vahlen.

Kaplan, R. S. (1998). *Advanced management accounting.* Englewood Cliffs, Prentice Hall International.

Kaplan, R. S., & Norton, D. P. (1996). *The balanced scorecard: Translating strategy into action.* Harvard Business School Press.

Kislingerová, E. (2007). *Manažerské finance.* 2. vyd. C. H. Beck.

Kralicek, P. (1993). *Základy finančního hospodaření*. Linde.

M. Vlčková, *Controlling as a Business Process Management Tool*, Contributions to Finance and Accounting, https://doi.org/10.1007/978-3-032-27526-4

Konečný, M., & Režňáková, M. (2005). *Controlling: (pro obor Podnikové finance a obchod)*. Akademické nakladatelství CERM.
Král, B. (2010). *Manažerské účetnictví*. Management Press.
Král, B. (2019). *Manažerské účetnictví*. Management Press.
Lazar, J. (2012). *Manažerské účetnictví a controlling*. Grada Publishing.
Lussier, R. N. (2019). *Management fundamentals: Concepts, applications, and skill development* (9th ed.). SAGE.
Mcwatters, C., Zimmerman, J., & Morse, D. (2008). *Management accounting. Analysis and interpretation*. Pearson Education Limited.
Mikovcová, H. (2007). *Controlling v praxi*. Vydavatelství a nakladatelství Aleš Čeněk.
Mocanu, M. (2014). Towards a definition of controlling. *Studies and scientific researches. Economics edition*, *0*(20), Article 20. https://doi.org/10.29358/sceco.v0i20.295
Petřík, T. (2009). *Ekonomické a finanční řízení firmy*. Grada Publishing.
Popesko, B. (2009). *Moderní metody řízení nákladů*. Grada Publishing.
Popesko, B., & Papadaki, Š. (2017). *Moderní metody řízení nákladů*. 2. vyd. Grada Publishing.
Preissler, P. (2020). *Controlling* (15th ed.). Franz Vahlen.
Reichmann, T. (1997). *Controlling: Concepts of management control, controllership, and ratio*. Springer-Verlag Berlin.
Růčková, P. (2021). *Finanční analýza: metody, ukazatele, využití v praxi* (7. aktualizované vydání). Grada Publishing.
Stoner, A. F. J., Freeman, R. E., & Gilbert, D. R., Jr. (1998). *Management*. Prentice-Hall of India Pvt. Ltd.
Synek, M. (2011). *Manažerská ekonomika*. 5. vyd. Grada.
Šoljaková, L. (2009). *Strategicky zaměřené manažerské účetnictví*. Management Press.
Šoljaková, L., & Fibírová, J. (2010). *Reporting*. 3. vyd. Grada Publishing.
Šiška, L. (2007). *Vybrané kapitoly z controllingu*. 1. vyd. Masarykova univerzita.
Vlčková, M. (2020). Controlling in relation to division of enterprises and company size. *IDIMT-2020, 28th Interdisciplinary Information Management Talks*, Sept. 2.-4., 2020 (pp. 369–376). Kutná Hora, Czech Republic.
Vlčková, M. (2020). *Účetní principy a postupy*. Wolters Kluwer. (v tisku).
Vochozka, M., & Mulač, P. (2012). *Podniková ekonomika*. Grada.
Vollmuth, H. J. (2004). *Nástroje controllingu od A do Z*. Profess Consulting.
Žůrková, H. (2007). *Plánování a kontrola: klíč k úspěchu*. Grada.

MIX
Papier aus verantwortungsvollen Quellen
Paper from responsible sources
FSC® C105338

If you have any concerns about our products,
you can contact us on
ProductSafety@springernature.com

In case Publisher is established outside the EU,
the EU authorized representative is:
Springer Nature Customer Service Center GmbH
Europaplatz 3, 69115 Heidelberg, Germany

Printed by Libri Plureos GmbH
in Hamburg, Germany